To. Colin

Lots of Love, always

Jeanette.

x.

LUCKIER
THAN
MOST

LUCKIER
THAN
MOST

*An autobiography
by
David Tomlinson*

A John Curtis Book
Hodder & Stoughton
LONDON SYDNEY AUCKLAND TORONTO

British Library Cataloguing in Publication Data

Tomlinson, David.
  Luckier than most.
  1. Acting – Biographies
  I. Title
  792.028092

  ISBN 0-340-53484-2

Published by Hodder and Stoughton,
a division of Hodder and Stoughton Ltd,
Mill Road, Dunton Green, Sevenoaks, Kent TN13 2YA
Editorial Office: 47 Bedford Square, London WC1B 3DP

Designed by Behram Kapadia

Photoset by E.P.L. BookSet, West Norwood, London

Printed in Great Britain by St Edmundsbury Press,
Bury St Edmunds, Suffolk

For Audrey

CONTENTS

ILLUSTRATIONS

The football match in *Bedknobs and Broomsticks*
   (© *The Walt Disney Company*)
In *The Love Bug* (© *The Walt Disney Company*)
More wizardry for Disney Studios
   (© *The Walt Disney Company*)
The whole family in California
   (© *The Walt Disney Company*)
Willie at six
Willie presenting his handmade trug to the Princess Royal
Directing Peter Sellers
Song at Twilight in South Africa
Luckier than most

CHAPTER ONE

*In which
I am born
into a family
steeped in
mystery…*

Some years ago my brother Peter was on his way to Heathrow on an airport bus. It was, I suppose, pure chance that the traffic stopped at Chiswick. Glancing sideways Peter was astonished to see our father sitting up in a strange bed, in a strange house, drinking a cup of tea.

My father was a solicitor and he lived by a very strict routine. He would arrive at our home in Folkestone on Friday night and stay until Monday morning, when, if truth be told, we were quite pleased to see him go. The rest of the week he lived in London – at the Junior Carlton Club, he said, although as we were seldom able to contact him there we had our doubts. Peter's discovery set me on the trail of the truth. Just what was Father up to from Monday to Friday? By the time all was revealed I was acting in London and far removed from the tensions and friction of the household which seemed to me to have plagued my childhood. The quest for information became an obsession. I was determined to solve the mystery. Did "our father which art in London" have a secret life? We always referred to him in that rather disrespectful fashion, but then a certain amount of filial disrespect seems to have been inherited.

The earliest of our Tomlinson ancestors whom my eldest brother Michael, the family historian, has been able to pinpoint with certainty was Richard Tomlinson, who lived in Battersea, London in the early nineteenth century, when it was still a place of gardens – both of the market and pleasure variety. He was apprenticed to a boatman called William Hollingsworth and became a boatman himself in due course. The training was lengthy (seven or eight years' apprenticeship) and very arduous. As there were only three bridges across the Thames at that time the river traffic was copious. His son William followed in his father's wake and was granted the freedom of the river by the time he was twenty-four. That year he competed in the 119th annual rowing race for Thames Watermen – the prize being the Doggett Coat and Badge. That was, I suppose, our family's first tenuous link with show business.

Thomas Doggett, an actor who had made his reputation playing low comedy, instituted the race in 1715 in honour of the first anniversary of the accession of the Hanoverian George I to the throne of England. The proclamation read thus:

> This being the day of his Majesty's happy accession to the throne, there will be given by Mr Doggett an Orange Colour Livery with a Badge representing Liberty to be rowed for by six Watermen that are out of their time within the year past. They are to row from London Bridge to Chelsea. It will be continued annually on the same day forever.

And indeed so it has, except now the Coat is red and not orange. Doggett was being neither entirely philanthropic nor indeed totally interested in sport. He was an actor, not averse to a spot of publicity, and moreover he was joint manager of the Drury Lane Theatre. The Thames was then the highway of London and, like the taxi drivers of today, the Watermen were responsible for getting a goodly number of patrons to the theatre – and preferably, Doggett most likely hoped, to *his* theatre.

So, on August 1st, 1834 my great-grandfather William set out an hour and a half before the tide rose, in the company of five other young men, to race against the tide in heavy wherries. He won by more than two lengths but it was touch and go for a while. His father, who had doubtless trained young trained young William for the race, followed the action in a boat rowed by eight oarsmen. While he shouted vociferous encouragement to his son, the oarsmen managed to collide with another boat and Richard was pitched head first into the river. William laughed so much at the spectacle of his submerged and sputtering parent that he nearly lost the race. Nevertheless, recovering he accepted with pride the Orange Livery and the Silver Badge – which remained in the family long enough for my father to remember wearing it at fancy dress parties but has now alas disappeared.

One of William's first recorded commissions as a Lighterman, which set him on the road to prosperity, was to remove the debris left by the conflagration which in 1834 resulted in the almost complete destruction of the House of Commons.

For a time William was engaged in boat building at the Adelphi Wharf but, despite the opposition of the Worshipful Company of Watermen and Lightermen who saw a threat to their employment, bridges were beginning to sprout across the Thames. When steam came William shrewdly abandoned building boats and turned to buying land and building houses. We think that his wife Betsey, who ran a most successful greengrocer's shop close by St James's Park, planted the seed money for his projects. To support this theory there is a story that her husband lost £1000 when a bank failed.

"Never mind," said sweet and fond Betsey, "I will make it up for you." And she did.

He built over three hundred houses in Hammersmith before moving on to Chiswick. In one of these, descendants have lived to this day. He ended his days as a gentleman of property.

Three sons survived him and his legacies point to a certain amount of family friction. Charles, the eldest, who had been packed off to Canada because of his insolence, didn't even turn up for the funeral. He was left his father's clothes, a mere one hundred pounds and an annuity of three pounds a week on condition that he didn't challenge the will or annoy his stepmother. (Dear Betsey, the mother of the boys, had died in 1876. William then married a rather well-off widow who annoyed him when she died by leaving all her money to her solicitor and a maid. He then took a housekeeper, Emma, who was reputed to be extremely ugly but jolly good at managing a house. He married her and as she was thirty-two years his junior, she lived on as his widow for another twenty-two years.)

The second son, Robert, despite having emigrated to America where he said he fought the Indians with General Custer (although presumably not joining him at his last stand) and despite continuing to behave like a cowboy on his return to England, going so far as to carry a six-shooter, did much better from the will. He was to receive income from a half-share in the substantial estate but most likely did not do so as he sold out to my father and uncle. It seems, however, that he spent a good deal of this on the demon drink. He was driving his brother (my grandfather) and my father, who was then about eight, in a horse-drawn carriage to Lords to watch the cricket when a policeman stopped him and charged him with "furious" driving! On closer inspection an allegation of drunkenness was added. Robert duly appeared at the court at Marylebone before a stipendiary magistrate, Mr Plowden, who fortuitously was not always on the side of the police. Years later when he practised as a solicitor in his own right, my father learned that this was because Plowden had occasionally been at the receiving end of the strong arm of the constabulary in his younger days at university when the forces of law and order had been less than appreciative of the high jinks to which, like many students, he was prone. As a very young schoolboy in the early eighteen nineties, my father was impressed with his first view of British justice.

In those days, defendants were not permitted to give evidence on oath. In the case of great-uncle Robert, this was just as well. They could, however, make an unsworn statement from the dock. Robert wisely declined that option but he was of course called on to plead to the charges and must have presented an uneasy spectacle as he stood in the focal point of the courtroom. Before his case was called, my father was reassured to see Plowden deal kindly with a crippled woman who had been charged with being drunk in the street. It seemed that the police might have tossed a coin as to whether they charged her with that or begging because when she asked for her matches back, Plowden berated the hapless arresting officer and discharged the lady with kindly words.

Surely that would augur well for Robert whose American accent could easily be confused by an overworked policeman for slurred speech so often associated with intoxication. His case, however, was not such plain sailing but apparently my grandfather made an excellent witness, regaling the court with his brother's experience with General Custer and stressing that the laid-back accent was caused by no influence other than America. Plowden gave Robert the benefit of the doubt but drily observed that he had seldom seen "a finer impersonation of a drunken man than that given by the accused!" My father was never to tire of telling this story. He never forgot Plowden who had a reputation for caustic asides, dubbed "Plowdenisms" by the legal profession. His acquittal remark to great-uncle Robert was said to be a classic Plowdenism.

It seems that Richard, the youngest son and my grandfather, was the blue-eyed boy. He and his wife Sarah did very well indeed from the will. As an architect and auctioneer, he ran the family estates and on his father's death became executor and trustee. Unfortunately he then proceeded to run the estates right into the ground with the encouragement of a dishonest solicitor. He lived extravagantly off the capital much to everybody's chagrin, including mine. Had he been provident, I too today might have been a gentleman of property! Instead he went bankrupt and ran off with a lady friend to the south coast, which shouldn't really have surprised anyone, as he and my grandmother had a notoriously volatile relationship, often hurling the lunch at each other or out of the window before retiring to bed for the rest of the day. My grandmother insisted she found having children distasteful and a tedious business, but the afternoons of reconciliation which followed the morning rows resulted in three: my uncle Dick, a daughter Sarah Gertrude, and my father Clarence, who was generally known, as is the fate which befalls Tomlinsons, as Tommy.

Uncle Dick married the daughter of a wealthy landowner, amongst whose assets was the John Bull pub at Chiswick, and moved to Henley-on-Thames before his father's notorious defection but was called back by his mother and sister to make what he could out of what remained of the estate. "Not a lot," was his conclusion and the negligence and indeed fraud he uncovered only increased his dislike of his father. My father's opinion of his father was always more temperate than his brother's but he was astonished and upset when Richard failed to pay for him to be articled to the Mildenhall solicitor, Odden Read. Sarah raised the hundred guineas necessary to set him on the road to his career. His time at Mildenhall, so close to Newmarket, also set him on a lifetime's interest in horse racing which he was always somewhat reluctant to admit.

Sarah was a delightful and good-natured girl and as far as I know the only member of our family to precede me on the stage. I treasure several photographs of her. She married the actor-manager Lauderdale Maitland and toured the provinces with him. She acted under the name of Gertrude Valentine but her career and life were tragically brief. In 1907 she fell ill and was diagnosed as having typhoid. As she lay in bed weak and dying Father asked her if she would like a glass of champagne. Three years separated them and they were very devoted to each other. He, a 23-year-old impecunious articled clerk, managed to scrape together enough money for a bottle which she managed to sip. From then until his death he could never talk about the grief he felt at her death. It had not been typhoid at all but an undiagnosed appendicitis which ended her life at twenty-six. Her 29-year-old widower went on to marry the actress Janet Alexander. He had a long career. He played at the Lyceum Theatre in many leading roles from 1908 to 1915 including Romeo, King Charles in *Nell Gwynne* and Ivanhoe. Subsequently he managed the Coronet Theatre in Notting Hill Gate. What could have become of the blessed Sarah had she lived?

My father was pure English and my mother equally pure Scots, although she was born in Calcutta. We are convinced (here again due to Michael's diligent researches) that we are descended on the maternal side from Lord Robert Stewart, the illegitimate half-brother of Mary Queen of Scots. Mother's paternal grandfather was the chaplain of the Scots kirk in Calcutta and his four sons became tea planters up-country in the Dooars. One of these sons, Henry, married my grandmother who was also his second cousin. But the life of a tea planter's wife in the intemperate climate with all sorts of diseases raging did not suit my beautiful and accomplished grandmother. She soon took her daughter, Florence, and a helpful Indian ayah back to Britain. My mother remembered virtually nothing of her father who died when she was nine, of a heart attack as he finished a game of polo at the Rangamutti Club. He was only forty. All she remembered of India was what she was taught by her ayah who called her Toto – a nickname that stuck with her for life. She also retained a Bengali song learned from her and used to sing it to my brothers and me.

> Jilly minny puddiah
> Na neena Nadiah
> Ek pice a hubble bubble
> Do pice a ghos.

Except for "Ek pice" and "Do pice" (one and two small Indian coins), the meaning of the song is lost to us. But we liked to chant it.

Grandmother, a particularly fine-looking 32-year-old

widow, did not exactly fancy existing on the modest pension provided by the tea company and set about finding a new husband. Soon she married an elderly widower, Dr Armitage, who had a successful practice in Grosvenor Street and children nearly as old as she was. Because he was also connected professionally with the German Embassy, Toto was sent off to finishing school in that country when she was nineteen. She always insisted that one day when out riding she met the Kaiser who stopped to converse with her. It is not all that unlikely. She was a beauty.

"And his English was excellent," she maintained.

That same year death struck once again and for a second time Grandmother was widowed. Unfortunately little money came her way from the doctor's estate which his sons inherited. One of these step-brothers to my mother was Sir Cecil Armitage, later to govern Gambia and subsequently to commit suicide on retirement near Cirencester; the other was Commodore Albert Armitage of the P&O and second in command of Captain Scott's first Antarctic expedition. Though she was still attractive her chances of a third marriage in her mid-forties (although she never gave up the pursuit) were realistically not so good. She concentrated on her daughter's, and took over the management of a bridge club in Dover Street which provided the two of them not only with bed and board but also with a very respectable circle in which to mix and hopefully to find a match. Toto was certainly not short of suitors but then, unfortunately from Grandmother's point of view, Clarence Samuel Tomlinson made his entry into her life. He would often later tell us that he was Secretary of the "Public Schools Dance Club" and it was at one of these functions that he met our Mama – at the Savoy Hotel. They were introduced, they danced and from then onwards she would have no other. In later years he used to tease us by telling us that they met on the top of a bus. As children will, we quite seriously believed this until persuaded, to our disappointment, that it was a joke. Toto's mother was considerably less than delighted with the match

her 23-year-old daughter was determined on. She had hoped
for bigger and better fish. Indeed Toto had been engaged
briefly to the heir to a peerage. This was the future Lord
Borwick, whose son George was later to be one of the
backers of *Boeing-Boeing*.

My father was about five foot ten in height. He dressed
neatly and with great simplicity, always sombrely in dark
grey, navy blue or black. I always felt that he was good
casting for a duke. He had great charm and was very popular. He was also devoid of foibles in regard to appearance, no
jewellery except later for a most beautiful platinum and blue
enamelled Cartier pocket watch given to him by a grateful
and generous client. He lost it but that was his way. He lost
most things and it didn't ever seem to worry him. He was
not at all acquisitive. He was undoubtedly good looking and
he certainly appealed to women. He was once told by a 17-
year-old girl friend of my brother Peter that he had got "SA".
He had never heard the expression before but he was absolutely delighted. Mysteriously – at least by the standards of
today – I suspect that he was secretly ashamed of his education or rather, as I think he saw it, his lack of it. He used to
say that he had been to the King's College School, Wimbledon, and then rather vaguely assert that he had finished "up
at Heidelberg". He would always just stop himself from
actually saying University. In fact he was at Neuenheim
College, run on the lines of an English public school with
mainly English pupils. Constance, Oscar Wilde's widow, to
escape the limelight, sent her two children by Wilde to the
school at much the same time as Father. Michael had found
no record to substantiate the claim that William John had
attended Christ's Hospital in the eighteen twenties. This
annoyed my father who went to extraordinary lengths to
establish the fact, with no success. "You put me to a lot of
trouble there," he would say crossly to Michael. In truth the
school William John attended at that time was the Bluecoat
School still standing today in Westminster for "fifty poor
boys of the parish". Later he was to chide me for sending my

eldest son to a grammar school. In any event, something pointed him as a young man towards the "Public Schools Dance Club" and consequently to my mother.

Toto was very much in love. They were married at St George's, Hanover Square on June 26th, 1913. The newly married couple took rooms in Kensington where nine months after the wedding their first son, my eldest brother Michael, was born. Father was in partnership with another solicitor but it was a young practice and not exactly thriving. He and Toto continued to live in rented rooms, moving to Addison Mansions behind Olympia where their second son, Peter, was born in 1916.

The war had been raging for two years and the British Government decided it could no longer rely on volunteers to beat the Hun. My father, to his great credit, volunteered before the draft was instituted. He left the legal practice to his partner and joined the army. He was commissioned in the Royal Army Service Corps and posted to the western front. At this point Mother, her two sons and an elderly nanny descended upon my father's brother, my Uncle Dick, and his wife Aunt May in Henley. Fortunately, as they had two sons of their own, it was a largish house – indeed the only one in St Andrew's Road that boasted its own garage. (I went to look at it the other day. It has now been split into two and the garage has disappeared.)

Aunt May was a kind and delightful woman with a clear soprano voice. She entertained the children. Her particular speciality at that time was "There are Fairies at the Bottom of Our Garden", a concept that quite inexplicably terrified my brother Michael to such an extent that even now he vividly recalls avoiding the farthest reaches of the Henley plot.

Across the road, behind a tall, forbidding wooden fence, lived Mrs Scott, the mother of the Captain who had perished in the Antarctic three years before. This was Scott's second expedition which Uncle Albert Armitage had not been invited to join. Mrs Scott too was avoided, but out of respect for the solitary lifestyle she chose.

It was there in Henley that I was born on May 7th, 1917, the day the United States War Department decided to send ten thousand army engineers to join my father in France.

CHAPTER TWO

Schoolday miseries,
home difficulties
and
adolescent yearnings...

Clarence Samuel Tomlinson (CST as we later took to calling him) returned from France invalided out with trench-foot and was posted to Shorncliffe in Kent, a camp founded inland and above Sandgate at the beginning of the nineteenth century to meet the threat of invasion by Napoleon. It was a fitting posting as one of the few subjects my father ever read about was Napoleon. He was fascinated by him and read his history repeatedly.

We left Henley to become tenants in a flat above Hudson's stores on the Sandgate Road. Thus began our long association with Folkestone. The next year we were in a hotel. A couple of other houses followed in quick succession. Although he was never much of a businessman, CST seemed to profit by their sales, for accommodation for his family got bigger and grander.

The first house I remember was at 2 Trinity Villas in the Sandgate Road. It was one of a group of houses which spilled out onto marvellous communal gardens. We moved there when I was four. I remember that I had been given a magnificently coloured large rubber ball. Experimenting with its bounce I went to the top of the house and dropped the ball over the banisters to the hall below. It disappeared completely. I ran down the stairs, searching everywhere, even down the steps into the road although I swore the door was closed. That ball was never found. I have never forgotten its mysterious disappearance.

Another childhood disaster was also hard to forget. I had a

little wooden boat with two rows of wooden sailors in it. CST one weekend – it must have been a weekend as he was only with us then – hired a motor boat to take us for a ride. This was a wonderful opportunity to test out my wooden toy. I hung it over the back of the boat so it could speed along behind us. Alas, it couldn't keep up and the string snapped.

"I can turn back and get it," the pilot of the boat assured me, seeing grief at the loss.

"Don't bother," my father commanded, "it's not important."

It was important to me but my father was an impatient man and he always seemed to be in a hurry. In fairness to him, possessions meant very little. Had the loss been his it wouldn't have bothered him at all.

CST was given to rages and could be very frightening. On one occasion he even managed to frighten himself. I must have been about eight when one day he found me in the nursery having turned on the iron. In a misguided attempt to teach me the danger he picked it up and slapped it down on my hand. The blisters welled up. My mother was hysterical and CST was suitably horrified by his irrational behaviour. I was rushed to our doctor and CST's explanation of the incident bore little relation to the truth. He blamed me, of course, and the doctor added insult to injury by telling me that I was a very naughty boy.

The truth is we were all frightened of my father, all except my mother who could and did oppose him on occasion; but generally speaking she was completely loyal to him and invariably supported him. He could always manipulate her to his way of thinking, however wrong or absurd it might be.

We, my three brothers and I, with her six grandchildren, have only the fondest recollections of my mother.

She was kindly, good natured and friendly and her family were far and away her major interest. She was very nice looking and always beautifully dressed. She was enormously well-liked by everybody and especially those who worked for us. She was also quite expert at running the house. Her talents were domestic and she was adept at all sorts of needlework – embroidery, *gros point*, *petit point*, crochet and knitting. I have a sweater that she knitted for me sixty years ago and I still wear it.

In most ways my mother was an innocent. Had she been wise in a worldly sense she would never have married my father. Suffice it to say she made a very good job of being a successful solicitor's wife. There was invariably tension in the house when CST was home for his weekends and our mother often seemed to be preoccupied. She had good reason. She was always caring but sometimes aloof and somewhat distracted. Father returned to his pre-war profession and had quite splendid offices in London's New Bond Street while Mother in Folkestone busied herself with the running of the house, her exquisite needlework (which Father rather denigrated) and bridge. Father approved of none of her social contacts and constantly tried to persuade her not to bother with them. As for our school friends, "Haven't they got any tea in their own house?" he would ask when he heard they had been invited.

Even as a small child I felt that there must be reason for my father's irritability and impatient gruffness.

Four sisters lived in the house and "did for us". They all arrived at the same time from Hythe, down the coast, where their father was a carpenter. Louise was the eldest. She wore pince-nez and looked forbidding but was very good and kind with all of us. Then there were Vi, Lena and Ethel. Vi and I shared a bedroom and as a small boy I adored her. As I have said my mother was often preoccupied through no fault of her own, but Vi was always available for me. She was wonderful, warm and affectionate. She would go off sometimes, rather wobbly on one of our bicycles which she couldn't ride, to see her young man, a bus driver. He was a splendid fellow whom she eventually married. But at this time in her life she was with us and always protected me from all comers.

"No, no, Mr Tomlinson," she would say when trouble

threatened, I thought with incredible courage. "You are quite wrong about that, Sir – David's a good boy." By this time it had been generally decided, certainly by my father, that I was the least favourite of his Folkestone sons. Later, when I shared a bedroom with Michael and Peter, Vi was not there to defend me. One night, after we had gone to bed, Michael and Peter had an absurd fight over a chamber pot. Michael had used it and put it under Peter's bed. Peter was not having this and pushed it under Michael's bed. Neither would budge and soon they were each grasping opposite sides of the pot, pushing it backwards and forwards and doing a sort of war dance. I thought that this was very funny, and so clever not to spill a drop. It was my laughter that CST heard. Having already decided that I was the cause of the disturbance before entering the room, he blamed me!

I was very happy to spend my time in the nursery and the large friendly kitchen with the sisters. Towels aired on the fireguard and there I listened to the four girls who were not averse to bickering – usually about money. Louise, it seemed, held the family purse strings very tightly. But Vi was my solace and I was away from the atmosphere in the rest of the house which I found intimidating, even though I was fond of my mother and even then was sorry for her. She lived somewhat of a life of fantasy and modelled herself on Mrs Darling. In fact both Michael and Peter had been so named because of *Peter Pan*. It was my mother's favourite play.

She was devoted to Peter, one year my senior, but it was Michael, my eldest brother, that I admired most. He always seemed so self-contained in an uneasy household. I was quite devastated by his removal to the Isolation Hospital for six weeks. Six weeks was an eternity. He had succumbed to the dread diphtheria, in those days a very serious matter. Although he seemed quite to enjoy hospital I was relieved when he returned and we once more took to the pleasures of Folkestone. There were horses and gas lights and Punch and Judy shows and a roller-skating rink. We would often skate and when we looked up to the Leas from the shore where the rink was and saw our mother, with Tinker the sealyham, waving to us we took that as the signal to get the lift up the cliff and return home for tea. On other days we could walk to the end of the Victoria Pier where concert parties performed and sometimes a deep-sea diver would disappear into the waters below. There were two ponds in Radnor Park – one for sailing model boats and the Peter Pan pond on which we rowed. We learned to swim in the heated indoor sea baths before venturing into the sea itself and most summer holidays were spent at home. We had a hut on the beach and spent all our days there away from the house until late evening.

Folkestone in those days was the kind of place where you knew everyone and they indeed knew you. Mr Muddle ran the grocery shop in Bouverie Road. He was very smart and wore a long navy-blue serge coat and over that a white apron tied twice around his waist and always a stiff collar and tie. When I was a child, walking down the centre aisle of his shop was a fascinating experience, rather like going to the altar in church. On either side, slanted biscuit tins lined the "avenue" to the far end. On one occasion when visiting the shop with my father, the temptation was too great. I lifted the lid from one of the tins and took a biscuit. CST went through the motions of being appalled. He confronted me with Mr Muddle and I was terrified.

"Mr Muddle, did you see what my son did?" he demanded.

"What did he do, Sir?" he enquired with a polite smile.

"He stole a biscuit," said CST.

Mr Muddle eyed me kindly. "Well, Sir," he said to my father, "I always say the children of today are my customers of tomorrow and if he wants a biscuit he can take one."

I was greatly relieved. No arrest. No prison. Dear Mr Muddle. He was a nice man and probably my first adult friend outside our immediate circle (apart from dear Vi).

We lived across the road from the Pleasure Gardens

Theatre where first-rate touring companies performed. My father, though as unimpressed with the stage as he was with literature or painting or indeed Mother's needlework, was impressed by success of any variety. Mrs Patrick Campbell arrived to play the theatre. Although much too old and overweight she was on tour in *Belladonna*. Jack Minster, the brilliant director of comedy, was on tour with her in this play. Years later he told me, "Yes, it is true. She was too old and overweight but any doubts the audience might have had about her when she first appeared were quickly dispelled. Her talent was so great that the audience were spellbound."

Father invited her to lunch. It is a matter of family history that I was perched on her knee, but I have no recollection of meeting the legendary actress.

Occasionally Father would bring one of his clients down to Folkestone for the weekend. One I remember was a very rich Irishman. He was an interesting man but I particularly remember him for three things he possessed which I coveted. He had a Cartier watch, a Rolls-Royce and a set of ivory brushes in a pigskin case. I hoped that one day I would possess such treasures. He was also a clever artist and I still have a sketch he did of me.

My elder brothers went first of all to a Dame School but I went directly to Feltonfleet School when I was seven. It was housed in a large building on the Shorncliffe Road (later destroyed by a flying bomb in the Second World War) to which I could walk with my brothers each day. It is surprising how once more the theatrical world touched ours. The headmaster of Feltonfleet was Claud Counsell, an amateur actor whose son John went on to found the repertory company at the Theatre Royal Windsor. I enjoyed my all-too-brief time there with my brothers. Although we were not noted for being particularly mischievous there was a time when the three Tomlinson brothers, standing on each other's shoulders (me at the top), managed to extinguish all the gas lights on the route. Our local bobby on the beat, whom we knew well, gave us a sound ticking-off and we

29

promised we would not do it again.

One day, walking back from school, I was bent double with an excruciating pain. An immediate operation to remove my appendix was performed but I remember only the initial pain and the subsequent most enjoyable convalescence at home in the spare room – it was a very grand room – and my mother nursing me. It was summer and I recall her in a shantung dress reading *The Water Babies* to me. It sent her into floods of tears. But then she cried very easily and enjoyed nothing so much as a weepy story or film. Inexplicably even a comedy would reduce her to tears. But perhaps even more surprising was CST's response to my illness. He arrived from London, full of solicitude and bearing gifts – a watch and a cricket bat. CST had a great dread of illness. His sister's demise at such an early age was always in his memory. And after all she had succumbed to the same complaint as afflicted me – peritonitis. But any illness brought out the best in him. It is true to say that the only time he was truly kind to my mother was when she was ill, so she made a point of being frequently ill and had, I think, two or even three unnecessary operations. That summer, bathed in parental concern, I could have understood why. I thought perhaps I ought to be ill regularly. However, fit and well I returned to Feltonfleet. But my father soon quarrelled with the headmaster and I was moved to a most horrible establishment. It was called Hillcrest School and was situated in Haywards Heath. The headmistress was at her best with visiting parents but the pupils loathed her. I've always held it against my father that he was a terrible judge of people – and it was certainly true in this case. Dickens would have been hard pressed to describe the sadism and brutality of Hillcrest. In the mornings we were lined up in a freezing corridor stark naked while Miss Hall, dressed in black clothes seemingly from Victorian times in the previous century, very lean and angry-looking with a pallid complexion and watery eyes, stood brandishing a cane as we were forced to jump into a freezing bath. She had an elderly woman friend who just seemed to hover about. They employed a schoolmaster who delighted in stripping the boys naked and thrashing them. A dreadfully unpleasant clergyman came to take us for scripture.

But Hillcrest was not only horrible by commission. What was omitted at the school was equally painful to a small boy. The headmistress, her cronies and her staff would sit at the top table of the refectory filling their faces while the boys had porridge and our own treacle – no milk. The one strong point of the school was blatant neglect of their charges. I still have a scar where I stuck a penknife through my finger – clean through from one side to the other. Miss Hall dismissed it as trivial and, calling on one of the other boys, said, "Oh, *Doctor* Hunt can deal with that."

Needless to say I learned nothing at that establishment – except perhaps to keep my head down.

Although Michael went directly from Feltonfleet to Tonbridge, my childhood was littered with academic establishments. I also attended another school in Folkestone where the headmaster, it is said, was noted for opening the Common Entrance Papers the night before the exam. Thus he made sure the students knew the contents. That headmaster was also noted for his parsimony. I later learned that my friend Robert Morley caused pandemonium when he was there by declaring, "Please, Sir, dry bread and treacle is not a pudding."

I was a less forthcoming child and usually managed to suffer in silence.

I was ten when I decided to be an actor. I remember the time and the place very clearly. It was at the extraordinary Pleasure Gardens Theatre which had been built by local Folkestone dignitaries as a petty Crystal Palace. It was the same shape but instead of glass being used the construction was of corrugated iron. It really was a most eccentric building. First it was an exhibition hall but the locals took no interest. Then it was turned into a skating-rink and that, too, was a failure. Finally they decided to build a theatre inside the vast arena and it was a surprisingly pretty one. I distinctly remember sitting there, all smarmed down in an Eton collar between my mother in a black lace evening frock and my father in a dinner jacket. The curtain went up on a very alarming scene. There in front of me was a deserted misty railway station and across the stage came the station-master swinging a lamp. It was Arnold Ridley's *The Ghost Train*. I was terrified and loved it.

"Do they really get paid for doing that?" I asked later.

Father nodded.

I couldn't believe anything could be quite so wonderful – and I decided then and there that it must be better than working and I have never altered my view.

It was that year I had my first experience on the stage. Canon Elliott, lantern-jawed, as good-looking as any actor, was the vicar of Holy Trinity Church. Most Sundays I went to his children's service. I don't remember God being mentioned much. His sermons seemed to be full of adventure and cowboys and Indians. He was a sweet-natured man who was decidedly stage-struck. He went on to become a King's Chaplain and the BBC radio priest. Sad to relate, he ended his days in a mental hospital.

Each Christmas he directed the children of Folkestone in a pageant which was performed on the stage in the ballroom of the Grand Hotel. It was a very exciting occasion. My brother Peter and I played Tweedledee and Tweedledum rolling about the stage in mock battle and Michael was the White King who separated us. Mother loved working on the costumes which she designed herself but had made up by her seamstress, Mrs Snelling, whose son, a newspaper vendor at the Central Station, greatly excited the town by marrying a millionairess. It was a real sensation. Later I played the lead in *Flyaway Land* at the Town Hall and appeared in my elder brother's shorts which were two sizes too large.

Christmas was of course also pantomime time and each year Murray King brought his company to the Pleasure Gardens. I was enchanted by him. He appeared as the Dame without teeth and was absolutely marvellous. He was also extremely successful – so successful in the provinces that he never bothered to play London. He was Widow Twanky in a memorable *Ali Baba and the Forty Thieves*. Mephistopheles appeared magically in a cloud of red smoke and then there was the most wonderfully glittery and beautiful fairy godmother. Perhaps the most popular were his well-known transformation scenes.

We didn't go to the theatre as often as I would have liked but there were cinemas aplenty for our amusement. I could walk to the Playhouse in Guildhall Street and the Central in the High Street where for sixpence I could sit in the front row of the upper circle (unusual in a cinema) and escape from home. My father still thought little of me and told me that I was hopeless and would never drive a car.

"My poor son," he would say, "what is to become of you?"

His own driving skill was never wonderful. He was erratic, impatient and always ground the gears.

Later other cinemas were built. There were the Savoy and the Odeon. I used to try to go every day. Four cinemas, all within walking distance, was my idea of heaven. There was also a fifth at Hythe. It was rather gothic and decorated with rustic timber. The manager of the Playhouse got so used to this solitary lad often turning up that he let me in for nothing. I was extremely grateful because the sixpences were not easily come by unless I had the good fortune to meet Colonel O'Halleron. Everyone, it seemed to me, came to Folkestone to die. Bath chairs crowded the promenades. Some were basket weave and the occupants could steer them but other, grander ones were wooden with windows that folded over and were manoeuvred by a companion or sometimes two – one pushing and one pulling. The occupants often looked in much better health than the pushers and the pullers. The retired Irish colonel was still on his feet and walked the Leas. He was afflicted with what I later learned was cancer of the throat which caused him to wheeze with the most extraordinary noise. You could hear him coming from a great distance. He was a dear man and every time he saw me, he would give me a half-crown. It didn't matter if I saw him twice in the same day. The half-crown was still forthcoming. He used to do this with all the children. I was forever on the look-out for him and it got me into the cinema. I simply adored films so long as they were American. I thought English films were absolutely terrible but American ones absolutely magical – especially if they starred Gary Cooper or Jean Arthur. For me, both were masters at making it look easy and I admired their talent and effortless charm. They are still my all-time favourites. The only part of a film to which I did not look forward was its end. It is perhaps ironic that the cinema, where I learned so much which helped me in later life, began for me as a distinct form of escape.

One day, I determined that the time had come for a protest. I had decided that my face did not fit. Michael was self-contained and perfect. He was always getting on with things. Mother was potty about Peter, with whom I was always scrapping in a brotherly way. When CST separated us on one occasion, he said: "Now Peter, don't you love your little brother Davey?" Peter looked at me through tears of rage. "Yes," he admitted, "but not much."

Then there was the baby Paul, dressed in silks and fussed over. He didn't get my reach-me-downs. Those would have been worn out as I had inherited them from both Michael and Peter. I made a decision. I did not belong. I composed a well-constructed letter.

Dear Mother,
I am sure I am adopted. I've finished with you all and leave you for ever.

I left this letter on the hall table and set off, spending the morning wandering around Folkestone. By lunchtime, I decided that I had punished my family enough and returned home picturing a distraught mother and brothers in tears of self-recrimination at having driven me to such a dramatic exit. I opened the front door expecting Mother to sweep me

into her arms in extravagant relief at the return of her little
ewe lamb.

"Oh, hello," she said as if nothing had happened. "Lunch
is ready and you had better wash your hands." She turned
and led the way into the dining-room. I could not understand the casualness of the greeting. Then on the hall table, I
saw the reason for her nonchalance for there, apparently
unopened and unread, lay my farewell note.

I don't think I ever seriously felt that I was adopted and
although few ever saw much resemblance between my
father and me, years later when my third son Willie was a
small boy, we could see a very clear likeness between him
and photographs taken of CST when he was a child.

It was true, I suppose, if my brothers are to be believed,
that I was the naughty one. I had an answer for everything,
even if occasionally I did stammer it out. One day I went too
far. I was cycling along the front promenade of the Leas, a
section where bicycles were forbidden. This was a fact of
which I was very well aware when a policeman stopped me.
For some reason the devil came over me and I kept on riding.
My rebellion resulted in my being summoned to attend the
juvenile court. The days that preceded my arraignment were
agony as I feared that I would soon be languishing in jail.
When the dread day finally arrived I found myself in front of
the magistrate who turned out to be our next-door neighbour and GP, Doctor Nuttall! My plight seemed to amuse
him, which surprised me – but I knew enough to keep quiet
and meekly accept his none too stern reprimand.

Eventually I followed my brothers to Tonbridge School
which I never enjoyed, not that I blame the school. Peter
urged me to try to learn to make friends.

"You're not very good at it," he said – and he was right. I
was a loner, but I do not think that all the hopelessness was
attributable to me. C. H. Knott, my housemaster, was in a
profession to which I think he was unsuited. He had been
at Tonbridge, gone on to University and come straight back
to the cloistered existence of a housemaster. He played

cricket occasionally for Kent. I was not one of his favourites.

All schools were pretty dreadful in those days.

On one occasion, Michael committed some misdemeanour and had to report to the housemaster's study. He expected to be beaten. However, Knott was entertaining A. P. F. Chapman, then England's cricket captain. Both were drinking from pewter tankards and looked cheerfully at Michael who, much impressed, thought hopefully that he had got a reprieve. Unhappily it was only a stay of execution. He was told to return the next evening when the master was on his own. He was beaten. The man's one and only attempt to beat me a few years later foundered. I told him that I had a bad back and that I was undergoing treatment. Tonbridge was at that time simply a typical English public school where not only masters but boys were encouraged to beat smaller boys. It was an example of the type of school which mystified foreigners. It certainly mystified me.

Years later, the Reverend Waddy, the then Headmaster of Tonbridge turned up at the Savoy Theatre where I was acting and persuaded me to visit the school. Reluctantly I did so. My housemaster was still there and did not appear to have aged at all. I had always promised myself that I would give him a piece of my mind if I ever had the chance but as is always or often the case in these situations when the opportunity presented itself, I did not take it.

For me there was only one good thing about Tonbridge. Leslie Howard's son, Ronald – "Wink" to his friends – was also there and one day on the edge of the rugger pitch, there stood one of my idols, dressed in a camel-hair coat. Only a sighting of Gary Cooper would have been as exciting.

"Why didn't you tell me? I would have introduced you," Wink told me. He didn't like school any more than I did but he viewed it with stoical acceptance as being inevitable. We sat next to each other in form and he became a lifelong friend. Later I was his best man when he married his beloved Jean. I always say he was bottom of the form and I was next to bottom. He thinks it was the other way around.

It must be said, however, that Michael thrived at Tonbridge, and later my younger brother Paul also did very well there. Peter, although he did less well academically, was liked by everybody. It is difficult to say why I was so hopeless but hopeless I was and I did not even look forward to the school holidays. I didn't get on very well with my mother as to some extent CST's negative attitude towards me rubbed off on her. However there was always the cinema at which I spent every possible moment.

By this time we had made our final move in Folkestone – to Wellfield Road. The four sisters had moved on and we had a daily woman, as well as a cook and maid who lived in. While I occupied myself at the cinema, Michael, who was always so clever and self-possessed, had for some time been interested in photography. He had set up a dark-room in the attic and used to say he wished he could exist on pills so he wouldn't have to interrupt his photography for meals. Somehow he managed to persuade two of the maids to pose in the nude for him. It had to be in the cause of art because only one of them could be considered a beauty, but perhaps it was just a voyage of discovery for Michael. Kate, the maid, was, to put it mildly, the less attractive of the two but I do remember when I saw the photograph being fascinated by the fact that one breast hung lower than the other – considerably lower. Disaster struck. Somehow my mother came across a print and exploded in horror. She always reminded me on these occasions of Marie Lohr, a lovely actress whom I was later to meet.

"What your father will say I cannot imagine," she kept repeating to Michael throughout the week.

I remembered once losing my glasses and that she had threatened me with the unspeakable horrors Father would inflict on his return home on Friday evening. My fear had been real although in the end nothing had come of it.

"Well, buy him some new ones," Father had said. He was certainly unpredictable. He could have his rages but they would be his own rages.

But nude pictures! And of the servants! This was serious and we were all worried. Partly of course for Michael – he after all was the miscreant on this occasion – but also for ourselves. The rage of our father who was in London would inevitably affect all of us.

After a very long tense week, Friday night eventually came, as did Father with his usual regularity. Mother, also a mistress of timing, did not meet him at the door with the news. Instead we sat through dinner hardly touching the food, waiting for the moment when all would be revealed.

After dinner, CST sat in front of the fire reading the evening papers, his feet up on the fireplace. Mother entered the room and standing in front of my father thrust the photograph at him saying, "Tommy – what (another wave of the print close to his nose) – what do you think of this?"

He was startled. "What is it, darling?" he asked nervously holding the picture at arm's length.

"Well look, Tommy. What do you think it is?" she insisted.

By then CST showed extreme nervousness. "I have absolutely no idea," he said. He then adjusted his bifocals and was relieved to note that as far as he could remember, the girls depicted had nothing to do with him.

"Don't you recognise Louise and Kate?" Mother again insisted.

"Louise? Kate?" he asked querulously.

"Yes, Louise and Kate," she raised her voice. "Louise the cook and Kate the maid."

Father took a close look. "Good God, so it is," he said.

"And who," mother drove on, "who do you think took that photograph?"

With some relief our father knew for certain that it wasn't him. On the sofa behind him Michael, not quite eighteen, squirmed nervously.

"No idea," said CST.

This was it. At last she delivered the punch line and Marie Lohr would have been proud of her. "Your son Michael," she said pointing at him with an accusing finger.

CST looked over his shoulder at Michael, turned back to study the photograph carefully and again he looked back at Michael. His words were unexpected to say the least and spoken with admiration. "Jolly good, old boy. Do an enlargement."

Mother was speechless. We sighed with relief. Sad to say, I was never allowed to see the picture again. I just vividly remember those uneven breasts and that her name was Kate. Both girls stayed with us for years and they were as nice as could be. However, Michael never got a second chance to photograph them in the nude.

By the time I escaped from school Michael and Peter had digs in London though they, like CST, returned to Folkestone each weekend. Michael was a clerk in the share registration department of Phoenix Assurance in King William Street in the City earning all of thirty shillings a week and Peter was working in the accounts department of P&O. Father announced he had obtained a job for me as well – he had a lot of contacts in London.

"You will be working at Shell-Mex," he told me.

The idea of putting on a stiff collar and tie every day and catching the early train to London to work in an office appalled me.

I plucked up courage. I had already made up my mind and that bolstered me. I had plans of my own.

"I'd like to be an actor," I said.

"Be an actor?" my father said. "Good God, you can't even speak."

But I was determined that my stammer as well as my father's opposition could be overcome.

CHAPTER THREE

*In which
I leave the army
and arrive
on stage...*

I had a little bit of money saved up from birthday and Christmas presents throughout my childhood and deposited in Glyn Mills bank which was not far from the Whitehall Theatre. I found a very small, very cheap, windowless room near Charing Cross. It would of course only be temporary – just until I had a starring role in one of London's theatres. I began to make the rounds of theatrical agents who, to my astonishment, had not been sitting there awaiting my knock on their door. My knowledge of the art of acting might have been keenly honed – all those years at the cinema learning from watching were certainly not wasted – but apart from Canon Elliott's children's pageants my actual experience was nil. I hadn't even acted at Tonbridge. No one had ever asked me.

I was fobbed off always. But there was a pleasure in those days I shall never forget – going to the Holborn Empire sometimes with my brothers to see Max Miller. To this day I marvel at his talent. He was the funniest man I ever saw on the stage and he had the audience in his pocket. He absolutely stunned them. I never heard anyone with such authority, such clarity, such wonderful control, and never before or since have I heard anyone get more laughter from an audience. The cheekie chappie stood alone mid-stage. He was the first stand-up music-hall comedian to change the traditional technique. He put his foot up on the footlights and addressed the audience personally. He was a riot and women loved him. There was a sense of danger about him and it was always thought that he would go too far. He never did when I saw him and these days his patter would be considered very mild. Later I was to meet him and I continued to do so whenever I played the Theatre Royal in Brighton, where he had retired. Every minute I spent with him was golden.

A month climbing stairs to offices only to be greeted with, "No thank you, nothing today" passed and I grew increasingly desperate in my windowless lodgings. My funds were sinking as quickly as my spirits. I couldn't go home and I would not admit defeat.

Coming out of the bank one day with the last of my meagre savings I passed the Central London Recruiting Depot. I must have passed it many times before without even noticing, but that day I paused and was greeted by a large sergeant-major who boomed: "Come in, lad," much as the witch enticed the starving Hansel and Gretel into her cottage. I wasn't actually starving but the day did not seem all that far off. So in I went. It was a question of facing home or the army and even the gruff sergeant-major seemed attractive to me compared with facing CST. Before I knew what had happened I was in the army – the Grenadier Guards to be precise.

It did not take me long to realise that I had made a mistake – a big mistake. The Foreign Legion would have been a holiday camp compared to life in the Guards. I spent six months at a recruit depot at Caterham where to say the discipline was rigid would be like saying the Equator is quite warm or that the monsoon season brings light showers to the tropics. The discipline in the Guards was spelt not only with a capital D but a capital everything else as well and usually set in italics. It was all spit, polish and drill. An order was an order. Nobody argued or even vaguely demurred. I was then posted to Wellington Barracks and what we did there was drill – and drill – and drill, apart from two weeks a year at Pirbright firing range. We were on guard duty at Buckingham Palace, St James's, and the Magazine in Hyde

Park and also at the Bank of England; each man got a new shilling when we were guarding the bank. When we weren't marching we were polishing. But I am grateful to the Guards for one thing. They taught me how to polish shoes. I am an expert at it.

I was, however, slightly saved from the full rigours of the regime by the fact that I was keen on cricket and rugger. These were the two things, the only two things, for which I had to be grateful to a public school background. If you were chosen to play for the depot you were excused duty for a whole day – so I played a lot.

After sixteen months I could take no more and obtained a discharge with good character for thirty-five pounds. I was grateful to CST who paid, having decided I should leave the army. And so it was back to Folkestone. I was still deter-mined on an acting career despite my lack of success in my brief time in London. Certainly Folkestone wasn't all that bad – compared with the army.

CST was hard-working and although he did little criminal work, preferring conveyancing (which he called "the lushy graft") and a lot of divorce, he rarely failed if he took a criminal case. It is certainly true to say that he was the right man to have on your side if you needed a defence. He was tenacious and he would work night and day to get the right result. Innocence or guilt mattered little to CST – acquittal was the only aim.

Michael once told CST that he thought a client was com-pletely innocent. Father's reply startled him.

"Not a bad thing. That's not a disadvantage."

While Peter was working for P&O he had joined the RAF reserve and during a three months' leave of absence from his job he trained as a pilot at Hamble. Soon after my leaving the army Peter escaped from his dreadful desk job, happily, for a short service commission in the RAF as Pilot Officer at the Flying Training School in Digby, Lincolnshire. Paul was still at Tonbridge and doing a lot better there than I had done in my time. He was a very clever and successful student.

Michael was articled to our father.

Although it was true I had retreated home, I was not without work. It might have been unpaid but it was work and the kind I wanted to do. I got myself into an amateur production of Sutton Vane's *Outward Bound*. In this play a varied group of people set out on their final journey, into eternity. It was directed by a remarkable and very talented woman, Mrs Sydney Kemp, at the Saltwood Village Hall. There were only two performances, on Tuesday and Wednesday night, for the benefit of local charities. Leslie Howard played my part in the film version. Now it may be well known that local papers seldom say derogatory things about amateur dramatic productions but perhaps my delight can be imagined when as a teenaged aspiring thespian I opened the *Folkestone Herald* and found just about the best review an actor can hope for:

> David Tomlinson was a constant source of surprise and wonderment. With all the polish and experience of a seasoned actor this amazing young man gave us a Tom Prior of which a man twice his years might have been proud. His easy confidence, nonchalant cynicism and expressive gestures conveyed everything necessary for the part and he won a richly deserved triumph.

Modesty does not prevent me from re-printing it. Could it be that at long last this was a small sign of what the future might hold for me? My family, however, remained unimpressed – though my father *was* impressed by the fact that I played the part without a stammer. To this day I occasionally get a letter asking me how I cured my stammer. For me the answer was very simple – tenacity and determination.

After *Outward Bound* I spent a lot of time with Mrs Kemp at her house in Hythe and she encouraged me to go ahead with my ambition.

"My instinct tells me that you will make a career for yourself," were her words which I never forgot.

I answered an advertisement in *The Stage* newspaper and

found myself unwisely in a very tacky company preparing to go to Edinburgh. I can't remember the play but I can remember that it was unrehearsed, unprofessional and unsuccessful and that the cast of five was abandoned in Dalkeith by the manager of the company who fled taking whatever money there was. One of the company he stranded happened to be his sister. He had neither family loyalty nor scruples nor, for that matter, sense because his sister knew where to find him. I used up the last of my money on the bus fare and went to his house on the seedy side of Edinburgh, only to have the door slammed in my face. I retreated but only as far as an enormous policeman I found at the end of this rather slummy road. The policeman, who happened to be ex-Scots Guards, was very large indeed. I told him the story of this man's dastardly behaviour and though he sympathised he assured me it was a civil matter. However, he offered to accompany me back to the house where the miscreant lived, thinking that his presence alone might just have some effect. Anyway his size gave me courage. The policeman was so annoyed at the manager's failure to open the door that he took to banging on it himself demanding entrance – "in the name of the law".

To my surprise and delight the door was duly opened and between us we managed to extract seventeen pounds from him. I hurried off to share it among the forlorn but delighted cast. Obviously it didn't go very far but I was received like the conquering hero.

So there I was left in Scotland, jobless but determined not to retreat to Folkestone and home. My mother's aunt Jean, who was also my godmother, lived in Edinburgh. She was a charming and surprisingly sophisticated spinster with a wonderful complexion and china-blue eyes. She was also rather well off but I was equally determined not to bother her.

"You must go home," she urged me.

I didn't.

I made friends with some fairly wealthy American medical

students from the university and shared their commodious digs for a while. They were exuberant company although I resisted their attempts to get me to accompany them to observe an amputation. What I needed was a job, not nausea. I answered another newspaper advert. This one called for a "pioneer Salesman". I envisaged trekking through the Rocky Mountains. Much of my imagination was formed by the cowboy films of my childhood and pioneer was an emotive word. The product, however, turned out to be Hoovers and the territory Edinburgh. I was put in the charge of a dear man called Bill Dolan, their top salesman. We were supposed to cover the tenements and put the hard sell on impoverished Scots wives. The front door was usually slammed in my face and on one occasion I was chased from the premises by an irate husband throwing parts of the cleaner at me. Quite naturally he resented the idea of his wife putting him in hock for six shillings a week for the foreseeable future. Luckily I was fleet of foot and managed a successful retreat. The Scottish did not care for my "posh" accent. Bill and I got on well, however, and for a time I stayed with him, his brother (who was a greengrocer) and their mother. I demoralised him and if it was a fine day we used to sit in the park in the morning and in the afternoon we would go to the cinema on my actor's card pass – one of the few perks at that time to actors, especially unemployed ones. Needless to say, I failed to sell a single vacuum cleaner and readily admit that it was through want of trying. Pride restrained me from admitting defeat. I wrote home to the effect that our show was so successful that the run had been extended. Michael, as usual, discovered the truth by getting hold of a Scottish newspaper and looking up the entertainments section. I returned to Folkestone.

During the closed season two of the professional actors from Arthur Brough's Folkestone company, David Bird and his wife Joyce, offered their services free of charge to work in a production of a play which I co-wrote with the then quite well-known actor Maurice Braddell. His mother, Lady

Braddell, was a friend of my mother's and when she heard that I was an aspiring actor she invited me around to meet her son. I was very impressed when he gave me a signed sepia portrait of himself and suggested collaboration on a farce he had in mind. Together we wrote a play with the unlikely title, *Give Us a Jangle*. I recall doing the rounds of friends and neighbours and borrowing furniture to dress the set and I also remember my brother Peter's inevitable shrieks of mirth from the fifth row of the stalls as the curtain rose and I was seen lying on a sofa in Joyce's lap with an ice-bag on my head. Although Maurice Braddell had a great success with *It's You I Want* which he wrote for Seymour Hicks, *Give Us a Jangle* disappeared without trace after a couple of performances in Folkestone.

Thanks to Mrs Kemp who recommended me, I became a general dogsbody in Arthur Brough's repertory company at the Leas Pavilion. The Arthur Brough Players were very popular in Folkestone especially at the tea matinees which took place on Wednesdays, Fridays and Saturdays at three forty-five. The tables which filled the stalls were meticulously laid, complete with starched white linen, and performing over the noise of the tinkling china and occasional, "Another cup, Maud?" was a challenge for any actor as well as an exercise in concentration. For the evening performances the tables and chairs were cleared away and the auditorium took on the guise of a conventional theatre. I was generally kept busy making tea and running errands, borrowing furniture and props from the local shops, but what I was really doing was watching – comparing actors and performances. I would say to myself, "He's good – he's terrible" and that was very important to me. It was the start of my training and I began to believe that I could tell the difference between what was good and what was bad. Arthur Brough himself, I decided, though obviously a nice man and a good and successful manager, was not a very good actor, unlike his wife, Elizabeth Addyman, who was very good indeed. She could have had an extremely successful career away from Folkestone but she put herself into her husband's hands.

Perhaps the most important thing I learned was that the vital thing an actor must have is courage. I have never changed my mind about that. When an actor walks onto that stage he has to be able to do it at that moment. It doesn't matter if he has a headache or his cat has just been run over or his wife has left him. He has to do it now. Not yesterday, not tomorrow – but now. That is really the only difference between an amateur and a professional. Amateurs can do it occasionally but the professional can and has to do it always. Through the years I have known some very talented people who lacked that one essential – courage. And I have indeed known some very courageous actors who lacked talent.

On October 5th, 1936 I played my first part on the professional stage. It was not exactly spectacularly taxing. The play was *Quality Street* by J. M. Barrie. At the back of the stage a window supposedly looked out onto the street. Five of us would walk backwards and forwards past the window, changing hats at each pass to give the impression of throngs of people. I distinctly remember hearing a loud guffaw from the audience as I made my first and only stage entrance without words. It was my brother Peter. Although the family remained unimpressed, as far as I was concerned it was a beginning.

As it was weekly rep we would open on Monday and the following morning start rehearsals for the next play. One Tuesday I began to rehearse the part of a dead body. The play was called *9:45* and billed by the management, as if they were rather unsure of it themselves, as "a mystery play or a comedy melodrama". Someone opened a cupboard door and out I fell, onto the stage. I did have rather long hair at the time and the audience may have been confused as to whether the body was male or female although I was billed quite clearly in the programme (which cost 2d by the way) as Howard Randall. I lay quite still on the floor for a very long time. At least it seemed a very long time as Arthur Brough, playing the lead of course, used to kneel not only beside but on me and perversely try to make me giggle.

In both these plays appeared a nice girl called Pamela Gordon. She was part of the Leas Pavilion Company for only a short time. Her mother was Gertrude Lawrence. I liked her a lot and it interested me that she was less than complimentary about her mother.

My progress continued. On November 2nd, the Arthur Brough Players presented Arnold Bennett and Edward Knoblock's *Milestones*. I was Thompson, the butler, and spoke my first line on the professional stage.

It was during this production that for the first and last time in my career I was "off". I had fallen asleep at home and missed my entrance. It was a salutary lesson. The depressing thing was that no one seemed to notice – either on the stage or in the audience.

The die, however, was cast. The theatre was, I had decided, to be my profession but it was by no means to be the whole of my life. I was rather envious of Peter being a pilot so I took myself off to the nearest airfield, Lympne, where I learned you could train for a modest sum. I can't imagine where the money came from as I was still the unpaid dogsbody at the Leas Pavilion, learning my trade. It didn't come from my father. He bought me a suit or two because he couldn't bear the thought of me not being properly dressed. Image was very important to him. A successful solicitor couldn't have a badly turned-out son.

I learned to fly on a de Havilland Tutor, a plane very similar to a Tiger Moth. My instructor was David Llewelyn who had made a record flight to South Africa. He was not only an excellent teacher but also a very kind and, most of all, patient man. I not only admired his skill but also found in him all the qualities I failed to find in my father. Although to this day I remain nervous of heights, I had absolutely no fear of flying at all. I must though admit to a slight frisson when David first put the plane into a spin, a manoeuvre necessary when learning to control a plane in an emergency. At a safe height, about five thousand feet, the aircraft is stalled by closing the throttle, pulling the nose up and then putting on full rudder. The result is that the plane goes spiralling down – round and round towards the ground. To come out of the spin you apply the opposite rudder and move the stick forward. The first time, as a pupil with David, I thought I would never be able to do it.

"It's the easiest manoeuvre you'll ever do," David Llewelyn said.

I was relieved to find that what I had been taught did indeed work. The plane came out of its spin. Some aircraft are very difficult to control but not the lovely old biplanes. They behave beautifully.

I soloed and got my licence before I was twenty. Not only did I love flying but the success did wonders for the confidence of the ugly duckling. My father, he who said I would never even drive a car, so hopeless was I, willingly admitted that it was a sort of achievement. But he still thought I should give up the notion of acting and get a proper job.

I was always grateful to David Llewelyn and was very sad when I later learned that he had been killed in a crash. He took off with a pupil and it seems the aircraft stalled and went straight into the ground. They never discovered what happened. Sometimes it is true that a pupil panics, grabs the controls and then freezes but, as I learned from an experience I had later, it would seem most likely that David fainted.

Somehow – and gratefully I have forgotten most of the details over the years – I next got involved in an entertainment called *Shoot the Works*. Forsythe, Seamon and Farrell, an American Burlesque trio, headed the cast. Forsythe, a dreadful singer, performed Joyce Kilmer's *Trees*, Hattie Seamon danced badly but the third member of the troupe was fascinating. Eleanor Farrell weighed at least twenty stone and at one point in the evening pushed a grand piano onto the stage, climbed on top of it and did an impersonation of a gorilla. She was riveting and also, off stage, an absolute dear.

I was the straight man, or so they told me, but my main job was to feed the comedian called Joey Porter. However, I was also required to sing and dance, two things I had never done before. The lyrics were no help and they linger in the memory as only truly dreadful verse can:

> We've got to open up the show with a bang
> Just to blow your blues away.
> We're tough, we're real hot stuff
> And if you frown we might shoot you down.
> We've got to open up the show with a bang,
> With a bang, bang, bang, bang, bang, bang.

Before this memorable number I had literally to open up the show. I parted the curtains and faced the audience. I was to pretend that the chorus had not arrived. In a badly fitting dinner-jacket with what the Stratford Empire audience regarded as a toffee-nosed voice I got the bird. I was very, very shaken. Luckily the chorus soon joined me from the auditorium and the show started.

Later dear Eleanor Farrell sought me out.

"Now listen, David," she said. "You just have to tighten your ass and get out there. You will always be nervous. You must learn to conceal your nerves. You must control them. Don't let them control you."

It was good advice. Mercifully, after a week at the Chelsea Palace and another at Chatham, *Shoot the Works* folded.

A Folkestone connection was to prove more profitable. The Rose-Price family lived in Hythe. Father was a retired general so naturally my father, always impressed by rank, was his friend. The general's son, Dennis Price, became an actor and to my great joy phoned me about a job going in London – at the Queen's Theatre. It was an understudy and walk-on but it was London and moreover it was John Gielgud's company . . . and what a company it was: Peggy Ashcroft, Richard Ainley, Alec Guinness, Angela Baddeley,

Frederick Lloyd, George Devine and of course Gielgud himself. There seemed to be no question of auditioning. I turned up and I was in. I couldn't believe it was so easy.

The play was *The Merchant of Venice* and I understudied Alec Guinness's Lorenzo as well as walking on in various scenes. In the trial scene with the Doge I stood stock-still stage left next to the proscenium arch, carrying a cushion on which perched a crown. I was paid three pounds a week to watch at close hand every evening Gielgud and Ashcroft performing wonderfully. Of course I was delighted with my good fortune. I lodged in Hammersmith at Sterndale Road – it cost me threepence to get to the theatre on a bus from Hammersmith Broadway. My dear landlady, Mrs Oliver, insisted on generously feeding me whenever possible, always pretending she had more food than she could use. She was impressed with my father who sometimes appeared on the scene in his smart American car, looking as usual like a duke.

There were five of us in the dressing-room at the top of the Queen's Theatre. Two, Hereward Russell and Alistair Bannerman, were killed in the war. There was among our number a very elderly Australian actor. He was about seventy which seemed to me at the time akin to Methuselah. He was extremely fond of cheap Australian wine which he let me taste. As I didn't drink, to my palate it was a lethal concoction and an experience not to be repeated.

The play was directed by Glen Byam Shaw and he framed the trial scene with the cast who needed to be very still. In the middle, at the feet of the Doge, sat the old Aussie holding the mace of office. One night he had over-imbibed the Australian brew. It is after all a long wait for the trial scene. The mace began to sway ever so gently at first as in a breeze. Then the mace holder took to turning backwards and forwards sharing his interested gaze between Shylock and Portia and then fixing on Bassanio, rather like watching a tennis match. The audience became fascinated and could not fail to focus attention on him. The trial scene was ruined.

Gielgud sent for him, presumably to give him the sack, but the Australian made an impassioned appeal to him.

"Oh, Mr Gielgud," he began before JG had the chance to say anything, "it isn't important what happens to me – that isn't at all important. But I'm desolate at having let my fellow actors down. I don't know what came over me. I'm so ashamed. I don't deserve to be on the stage." On and on he went excoriating himself until he had the kindly Gielgud almost in tears – never, it is said, a very difficult thing to do.

"Well, dear boy, please don't do it again," was all he could say.

That night the Australian was so drunk he fell fast asleep on the stage, sitting up, and he got no further reprieves. His consumption of alcohol was truly prodigious, unlike that of Dennis Price who was thought to be a drinker but in reality could not manage more than a couple of beers without finding himself under the table.

It was an eventful time and such a joy to be in great company. Although the critic James Agate said that he would be better suited to the role of Bassanio, Gielgud in my view was a great Shylock and the extremely handsome Richard Ainley (later to be badly wounded in the war) a charming Bassanio. Peggy Ashcroft was a wonderful Portia. Of course I felt that I could have played Lorenzo better than Alec Guinness. It is hard to believe now that at the time I thought he was decidedly wooden.

While I was impressed by the company in which I was seen Michael and Peter still thought I was dotty dressing up every night in a Venetian costume and standing stock-still holding a crown on a cushion. I used to see my brothers regularly and remained absolutely convinced I was doing the right thing. CST whose relations with me were improving as the years progressed, often had me to lunch at his club and occasionally reminded me that there was still an opening for a clerk at Shell-Mex. But I was a professional, albeit only just, and spent my time as ever watching and learning.

Thus my West End début was effected with surprisingly little formality. This contrasts starkly with the tribulations which face the newcomer to the profession today. Equity has, in effect, barred opportunity to those who do not have their "card" and does not readily give a card to any who have had no experience. Amongst the many who have faced this seemingly insoluble impasse with success are two of my sons.

I recall an occasion when a woman reporter phoned me to ask my views on a campaign being proposed by the Minister of Labour to discourage acting recruits in view of the considerable unemployment amongst them. I said I felt it would take more than this to discourage anyone who was really keen and that opportunities were always there for talent and always would be.

Next day in the newspaper, under the heading "Minister says don't Mrs Worthington", an allusion to Noël Coward's witty song, the formidable trio of Sir Ralph Richardson, Sir Laurence Olivier and Sir Donald Wolfit were quoted in favour of the campaign, lamenting much talent in the drama schools doomed to be wasted and unused. Mine was the only dissenting voice. Although I was quite unaware that these three theatrical notabilities had been consulted, I still feel I was right. Can anyone recall much coming out of the campaign? Perhaps Equity's discouraging tactics have succeeded where the Minister failed.

I was standing at the side of the stage at the last matinee of *Coriolanus* at the Old Vic and was astounded to see Laurence Olivier as the curtain fell, raise two fingers and blow a raucous raspberry at the audience.

"You are naughty," Sybil Thorndike chided him, and smacked his hand. I didn't understand quite why Olivier did this until nearly ten years later when making a film, *Fame is the Spur*, with the legendary Seymour Hicks. He said to me, "You must always have a modicum of contempt for the audience – not too much – just a little, and don't ever forget that none of them can do it as well as you."

I suppose Olivier was just registering his modicum of contempt.

When *The Merchant of Venice* folded I was off to North-ampton – famous for shoes and ever after, as far as I was concerned, for giving me my first proper acting job in the professional theatre at the charming Theatre Royal. One of the plays in the repertory was *Black Swans*. I had the part of a nervous youth. Oswald Dale Robertson was a character actor with the company. He had an enormous head and did look rather like Crippen. As I came off the stage he grasped my arm firmly.

"You'll be all right," he said.

I didn't know what he meant. I hadn't been feeling ill. But later he explained that I would be all right in the business and he liked my performance. The encouragement was very welcome and his friendship was wonderful.

Errol Flynn had not long since left the Northampton company when I arrived. By that time, he had just about made his name and had already begun to make his extra-theatrical reputation and the town was abuzz with rumours and gossip about his amorous adventures. Mrs Panther of Trueform Shoes was the guiding hand and financial cornerstone of the Theatre Royal. She, although of uncertain years, was said to have delighted in Mr Flynn's antipodean charms. Years later I asked him about her.

"She scared the hell out of me," he said.

Still she could be forgiven anything. She kept the theatre and its twice-nightly repertory solvent. My particular pleasure in Northampton was to nip along to the New Theatre and catch the last half-hour of music-hall after our curtain came down.

Tyrone Guthrie, a great man of the theatre, came to see a production. He stayed the night and on Sunday gave the company a lecture sharing the fruits of his theatrical wisdom. His dedication to the open stage and to Theatre in the Round never appealed to me. As a spectator I found it uncomfortable, and avoided it totally as a performer, but I shall never forget his witty, amusing and endearing talk full of backstage gossip and visionary ideas.

I'll also never forget that he asked me to come and see him at the Old Vic, of which he was then head, and the notion of a great classical acting career seemed to open up before me. Hamlet, Romeo, the Master Builder – I would do the lot. Watch out Gielgud, watch out Olivier, Tomlinson was on the move. But as was to become my wont, I clasped the bird nesting in my hand rather than seeking the two in the bush and accepted a firm offer of a tour in *George and Margaret*, this time under the very reputable auspices of Prince Littler. The original production was still running at Wyndhams. Irene Handl made an immediate success in this, her first role. She played Beer, the maid who comes on at the end. She never spoke and I don't remember ever seeing a funnier perform-ance entirely in mime. But the tour was not ready and I was first to understudy in *Quiet Wedding* at the Piccadilly Theatre. Francis Drake, a sweet little old man, was a fellow under-study. He was a very good actor but terribly, terribly shy. I've found that most actors are shy, particularly those who may appear less so. We had plenty of time together each night and used to stand on the roof of the theatre surveying the summer sky. I told him there would be no war but he usually disagreed. The fifteen-year-old Glynis Johns played the young girl in the play. She had been acting profession-ally for three years already. During my time as understudy she knitted me a sweater.

It was while I was understudying at the Piccadilly that my grandfather Richard died. Although he had lived to a good age (he was eighty-eight) I was very sad at his passing. Apart from my mother and Michael he was the relative I most liked until later years when Peter became very close. He was a great talker and had a lot to talk about. He had travelled widely and had been absolutely everywhere. He was far more interesting than my father and a great deal more patient. Of course, by the time I got to know him through his too infrequent visits he was done with the excesses of youth which had caused so much trouble in the family. When my Uncle Dick had discovered to what extent his father had milked the family estate, possibly with the aid of the ill-chosen solicitor, he threatened court action. It is a credit to my father, as a professional lawyer, that he would not allow it. Grandfather had been pensioned off and what remained of the estate was kept far from his grasp. By that time both his wife and his mistress had died and three doors away from him lived a wealthy spinster, Emily Wootton-Woolley, who fell in love with him. Both my father and grandfather seemed to have had a fatal attraction as far as women were concerned, although this time the match was very success-ful. He was attractive, witty and charming and she was very, very rich. It seemed to suit both of them and by the time I, as a young boy, knew my grandfather, he was married to this delightful lady and had mellowed into a charming, patient soul, no longer even likely to throw the lunch out of the window.

"Isn't it wonderful," his wife said to me on one occasion, "he's taking me to New York."

"He's doing nothing of the kind," my father corrected her *sotto voce*, "she's taking him."

The tour of *George and Margaret* opened at the Finsbury Park Empire on July 31st, 1939. I played Roger and we performed twice nightly at 6:40 and 8:50. I was making six pounds a week and I was in heaven. The White House restaurant, two minutes from the theatre, served marvellous dinners for two shillings. A hand-tailored suit cost four guineas. I was rich. A week in Finsbury and then I was off on the road.

CHAPTER FOUR

*Touring, filming
and astounding
my father while
the mystery thickens...*

Unlike many of my fellow actors whose eyes were fixed firmly on London, I absolutely adored touring. It seemed to be such a lovely way to spend one's life, travelling around the country and being paid for it.

I enjoyed the theatrical boarding-houses and the splendid ladies who ran them, usually it seemed for the sheer joy of it because they could never have made any money out of actors. Their husbands worked and what the actors paid would be something to add to the weekly budget but never adequately paid for what these ladies gave us. They always treated us as very important people and the suppers laid on round the fire after the show more than compensated for the cold linoleum on the bedroom floor and sometimes the pot under the bed. Of course, in each town they established their own hierarchy and bragged of former guests.

"We once had Ivor 'Novvelow' staying here," a landlady would say, proudly displaying the guest book in which a noted personage would have written great praise such as, "Thank you for comfy digs during Holy Week."

I even liked the threadbare dressing-rooms in the grand old theatres of the northern industrial towns which in themselves I found fascinating. An actor on tour has a lot of time on his hands, usually in a place where he knows no one. Some haunt art galleries, some the racecourses, and some play golf. Some spend their time in pubs and others take a keen interest in the *ingénue*. I spent my time browsing in antique shops . . . or more often in those days, junk shops. I had always, since my teens, had an interest in period pictures, anything old. Although I still don't concentrate on any particular period and would not call myself an expert, as I learned how to act from watching and listening, so I developed a kind of instinct for quality and what is intrinsically good – but it took time. Over the years it has been an everlasting pleasure.

I was in Shanklin, on the Isle of Wight, when on Sunday, September 3rd, Prime Minister Chamberlain announced: "This country is now at war with Germany."

The night before, my father had assured me on the phone there would be no war. We would have played Folkestone that week but the tour was immediately cancelled and I took the boat to Portsmouth where on the station platform the large bag containing everything I possessed was stolen. There I met Rob Wilton, the music-hall performer. He was on tour in *When We Are Married*. He was far more concerned about my lost bag than imminent war.

"Even a war doesn't stop the buggers," he sympathised.

Total blackout ensued, although the blitzkrieg which the government had expected to produce a hundred thousand immediate casualties did not. The West End theatres closed and the shops sold out of black curtain material. Road deaths doubled owing to the fact that officialdom had insisted that car headlights had to be blacked out with cardboard allowing only two inches of light to escape.

My younger brother Paul was undergoing flying training. He had, unlike me, passed through Tonbridge with flying colours and merited a King's cadetship to the RAF college at Cranwell. In fact, not yet eighteen, he was the youngest cadet when war broke out. Michael, never to complete his articles to my father, joined RAF Intelligence. His eyesight barred him from flying, although it transpired that he was in the air quite often during the war.

By November the theatres in London began to re-open.

There had been a much shorter hiatus as far as touring was concerned and I was soon on tour again in *Quiet Wedding*, playing opposite Sarah Churchill who was advertised as "Winston Churchill's daughter" which did not do a great deal for her already shaky self-confidence . . . nor indeed did it do a lot for the business. It did, however, give me a great boost in CST's estimation. Imagine, his son was working with Winston's daughter – although in truth he never much cared for Churchill. It was, somehow, still fame by association. But perhaps he was beginning to change his mind about me.

Sarah had fallen in love with the comedian Vic Oliver who was a very big star indeed at the time and showed her an entirely different life from the political world in which she had grown up. They had married against great family opposition. Although she adored him, or maybe because she adored him, the marriage did not make her happy. The new world to which he had introduced her and which she found so fascinating also provided him with a great number of temptations which he did nothing to resist. Nor did he attempt to make a secret of his dalliances.

Sarah was a sweet girl, very calm, very shy and controlled to the point of introversion. Her nanny travelled with her as companion and dresser.

The Queens Hotel in Leeds was newly and expensively refurbished.

"You'll be staying at the Queens, I suppose," Sarah said.

"Of course," I agreed, having had no such intention. Theatrical boarding-houses continued to suit me and my pocket very well. But I splashed out and for the first time as a working actor, I booked a room at the hotel. It cost ten shillings and six pence a night (I was making six pounds a week) but it was worth it. I still remember the stars on the bedroom wallpaper, the luxury of a private bathroom and nectarines for breakfast.

Sarah and I supped together after the show rather grandly in the hotel's opulent dining-room. Father eagerly joined us one night and she charmed him. Of course, just being who she was would have been enough for CST but she was also the ideal dinner companion. She was quite charming but sadly she was far from happy. After the show she always rang Vic and as often as not it resulted in tears, as the phone was sometimes answered by a female voice. What, she cried, could she do about his infidelity?

"Some wives put up with it," I told her. Sarah would have to decide for herself if she could. She, however, was too much in love with him to endure it and the marriage eventually ended.

When the tour finished Sarah gave me a white silk scarf as a parting present. I was very touched and she had been an ideal colleague.

We didn't meet again for many years, and although there had been an enormous amount of publicity surrounding her various escapades, her drinking and eventual decline, being faced with the reality was still a shock. I was attending the Cork Film Festival and felt a clout on my back. It was Sarah, withered, haggard and blind drunk.

"Hello, you old fucker," her voice was as coarse as her language. It was devastating to see what had become of the fastidious young woman from *Quiet Wedding*. In her memoirs she had written that I had come on stage during *Quiet Wedding* at the Coliseum wearing a fireman's helmet to protect me from the expected bombings on the day war was declared. As on that day I distinctly remember standing on Portsmouth Station having my bag stolen, I could not have been at the Coliseum – besides which I have never played the Coliseum. But, sadly, more than her memory had gone. Her person and her dignity were in shreds and she was asked to leave the hotel. She left together with her secretary and nurse. Poor Sarah.

Next I was on tour with *The Police Are Anxious*. The leading parts were played by Joyce Barbour, Ernest Thesiger and Frank Cellier who was scheduled to play the groom's father in the film of *Quiet Wedding* which Anthony Asquith was about to direct at Shepperton. Frank was a dear man and a very fine actor. He was also kind and generous. Not only did he give me help with my performance but he also took me to his house in St John's Wood. We would have supper there and talk far into the night. Perhaps at this stage I was looking for a father figure and he filled the bill nicely. Frank was alone and lonely at that time as his marriage had foundered.

Asquith came to see the production and to my great joy cast me too in the film of *Quiet Wedding*. I had already made a short film for the war office called *Name, Rank and Number*, the title of which is pretty self-explanatory. The purpose of the film was to warn the military that if taken prisoner that was all they were to disclose to their captors. It was meant merely for instruction with no pretence at entertainment. It made the rounds of the camps during the war. My brother, Michael, in Ceylon in charge of a number of things including entertainments for the troops, avoided whenever possible Ministry of Information films, considering the war ghastly enough without inflicting further punishment on the men. Films, he reasoned, were for entertainment and a bit of escape. However, finally in desperation he gave a copy of *Name, Rank and Number* which had been gathering dust to the projectionist and was astonished to see his brother on the screen. He did manage to avoid *Garrison Follies*, also directed by Maclean Rogers, who was noted not so much for his sparkling work as for his prodigious and continuous consumption of Guinness. His assistant's main task during filming was to keep refreshed his stock of the brew. There was always a bottle to hand, under his chair. *Garrison Follies*, made for Butcher's Films and Signet (the lowest of the lowliest producers at the time) was a musical comedy set in an RAF camp. Misunderstanding and mistaken identity ensue when they decide to stage a concert party and water carnival. It was hailed by *Today's Cinema* as a "cheerful, tuneful, light-hearted spectacle" but that was thanks to its stars, Barry Lupino and the extremely attractive Nancy O'Neil, rather than to any expertise on the part of Mr Rogers whose

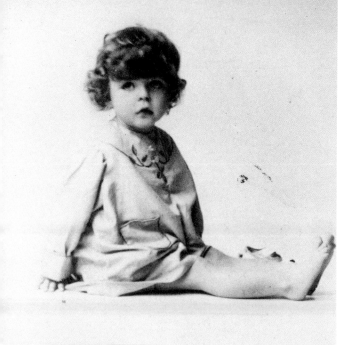

The author, age five, looking warily into the future.

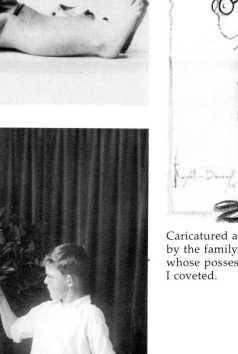

Caricatured at ten by the family guest whose possessions I coveted.

My first stage appearance – flapping about in hand-me-down trousers.

My mother's youthful beauty was irresistible.

CST was always happy if erratic at the wheel.

I was seventeen and preparing to solo at Lympne.

This is no costume. I trained in Canada for the war.

The Caucasian Chalk Circle at Northampton Rep. I never mastered the art of make-up.

Peggy Ashcroft, the eccentric Flower Lisle, my romantic interest in the film of *Quiet Wedding*.

Working with one of my heroes, Leslie Howard, magnificent on screen and off in *Pimpernel Smith*.

The beginning of a very beautiful friendship in *The Little Hut* at the Lyric Theatre.

Opposite above With Michael Redgrave and Basil Radford in the story of an RAF Bomber Station, *The Way to the Stars*.

Opposite below Meeting King George VI and Queen Elizabeth in the midst of a very starry line-up.

Three men out of their boat. I was waterlogged in the Thames with Jimmy Edwards and Laurence Harvey.

Wedding day – the beloved Audrey.

direction consisted of rather laconic instructions.

"Let's have a bit of life," he pleaded.

A group of extras formed a small crowd scene standing outside a church door waiting for the bride and groom to appear.

"Don't just stand there," he instructed, but he neglected to suggest just what these inexperienced performers might do so that when he called for action he was greeted by silence but one voice, after a long pause, was heard to shout, "Isn't Alf brown!"

Anthony Asquith was a marvellous and patient director even though his choice of a career seemed extraordinary considering his background. He had been brought up at Number Ten Downing Street while his father was Prime Minister. His mother, Asquith's second wife, was the eccentric society lioness Margot Tennant. She nicknamed her son Puffin because of the shape of his nose. It was a nickname in which he revelled. He did have extraordinary looks, similar to his mother, not only the hooked nose but also a mop of reddish-blond curly hair. He dressed in a boiler suit with a heavy leather belt around his waist.

Educated at Winchester and Balliol College, Oxford, his first and abiding love was music, but he accepted that he didn't have the talent to compose and threw himself into films with a single-minded energy. Because of his parents, he knew everyone. As a young man he went to Hollywood where he not only stayed with Douglas Fairbanks Senior and Mary Pickford but also discussed film technique with their neighbour, Charles Chaplin. He was the most unassuming of men. He nibbled his lips shyly before speaking with a slight stammer. He curled himself up under the camera as a scene was being shot in an attempt to make himself invisible. He was always eager to apologise for non-existent faults. He even apologised to inanimate objects. If he tripped over an electrical cable he said, "Sorry." Puffin Asquith had started with silent films in 1926 and by the time I worked with him he had already made his distinctive mark on the industry with the wonderful classic film of *Pygmalion* which starred Leslie Howard and Wendy Hiller. He was greatly loved and for years served as President of the Association of Cine Technicians.

Quiet Wedding had a very starry cast – Margaret Lockwood, Derek Farr, Roland Culver, Jean Cadel, Athene Seyler and of course Frank Cellier. Referred to by more than one critic as the "English Clochemerle", it was a fairly simple story. The couple to be married desire a simple wedding but the relatives intervene. I played Margaret Lockwood's brother John, hopelessly in love with the rather eccentric Flower Lisle, played by Peggy Ashcroft, then newly married to the lawyer Jeremy Hutchinson who was at that time serving in the navy. It seemed to me that she did not enjoy filming. Perhaps of course it was just nerves, or perhaps it was me. She was a very experienced stage actress, having by that time played not only Portia but also Juliet, Cleopatra, Lady Teazle and Rosalind.

But film acting as opposed to stage acting seemed to me to be a piece of cake. Little did I think then that by the time I was done I would appear in fifty films.

Quiet Wedding was filmed on one sound stage at Shepperton Studios. Within twenty feet of our wall an unexploded German bomb dropped one day, considerably interrupting the action. Luckily it remained unexploded while they removed it. My only other close shave during those early days of the war was off duty. I was living in Robert Adam Street in London, in a boarding-house near the Wallace Collection. I was returning there with a girlfriend when suddenly the air raid sirens sounded.

"Lie down," she shouted, throwing herself to the ground.

I was wearing a new suit. Not in this suit, I thought to myself. I dragged her to her feet and we continued on our way.

Despite the war the première of *Quiet Wedding* was quite an event. My mother and father came and CST was impressed – not only by my acting but by my salary. He had once visited the studios to have a look and he was bewildered. He couldn't understand it because as often as not on a film set nothing seems to be happening. The technicians are usually lighting and the actors sit around waiting or return to their dressing-rooms.

"How much are they paying you for doing this?" he asked.

I told him and he was astonished.

"You're living in a fool's paradise," was his considered reply.

Mother was more interested in the final product though equally bemused.

"Is that you?" she asked pointing at Derek Farr.

"No, dear."

"Is that you?" she asked five minutes later.

"No, that is Roland Culver."

And so she went through most of the film equating me with every male member of the cast. Even the identity of Bernard Miles was in question.

There was one last tour around my beloved industrial towns in those early days of the war before the necessity for military service closed in on me, and there was a film version of Fred Duprey's stage farce, *My Wife's Family*. It was I think the third remake. This one starred the very pretty Patricia Roc in, I believe, her first film. But before I joined the war there was the absolute joy of being cast as one of Pimpernel Smith's students. This film, now a classic, aroused national pride in the best possible way. Leslie Howard played Horatio Smith, tweedy, bespectacled, pipe-smoking professor of archaeology. He was the epitome of the absent-minded professor who turns out to be the mastermind behind an organisation dedicated to rescuing scientists and artists from Nazi Germany. As William Whitebait wrote in the *New Statesman* after the film's release:

The mingling of excitements and the battle for freedom

has been done with considerable tact; and party stupidity rather than private lusts is the line taken against the Nazis . . . *Pimpernel Smith* is a success all round for it romps home as an adventure which will thrill even devotees of Charlie Chan. Mr Howard has gauged his effects on audiences with some precision.

I was overjoyed to be working with one of my heroes. I had always greatly admired his screen appearances, I had watched him from afar as he visited our school, and now I was working with him. It was too good to be true. I avoided telling Leslie of my friendship with his son until the part was confirmed.

Leslie Howard was the producer, director and star and he had a good deal to say about the script as well. He certainly wasn't the romantic ethereal character people thought him to be. He was actually quite tough, although he had enormous charm; on the set he would stand for nothing less than perfection. He would set up the scene meticulously and then, at the very last minute before shooting began, he would step into the shot and play his part, making it seem the easiest thing in the world. I very greatly admired him.

CST came down to Denham while we were filming. He wasn't going to miss meeting Leslie Howard.

"Mr Howard," he said, "it is very nice to meet you. I always regard you as the perfect example of the best sort of Englishman."

"It is awfully nice of you to say so, Mr Tomlinson," he replied, "but I don't have a drop of English blood in me."

Yet, he *was* the archetypal Englishman on the screen, and a very great actor. He was a shining talent and had that rare quality shared by Gary Cooper – the ability to make it look easy.

I think it was no secret that Leslie Howard was a womaniser. Mary Morris who starred in the film was the object of his attentions, although it was fairly well known that her affiliations were to members of her own gender. Leslie seemed to regard that as a challenge to be overcome. She, a very sweet woman, rebuffed him gently.

My father by this time began to treat me with growing respect.

"I think you should use a different name," he said.

"Why?" I asked him.

"Well, Tomlinson. I don't think that that is a very good stage name. Why not call yourself David Drew?"

This suggestion left me utterly bewildered. The only Drews of any note were American and one American Drew had been a repertory player in this country. He had been a suspect in a murder case at Reading and although an inquest jury had vindicated him, it must have been a harrowing experience. Actors are superstitious by nature and had I wanted to change my name, I doubt whether I would have ever selected "Drew".

It seemed distinctly odd that CST would want me to change my name in this way. I could only infer that he did not like the idea of my using my proper name of Tomlinson. Years later, I discovered that I was right and also learned the reason.

At the end of 1940 I enlisted in the RAF, just a hair's breadth ahead of conscription. My experience in the Guards had made me very reluctant to get involved with the military again, but war was a different matter. This time I wanted to fly, but at first I was posted to Newchurch, not all that far from Folkestone. I was on radio location duty, tracking aircraft that came into English airspace. I longed to be a pilot. After all, I already had a flying licence.

In 1939 Peter was posted as pilot and personal assistant to Air Vice-Marshal Arthur Harris – Air Officer Commanding 5 Group. Later he volunteered for operations and was posted to 3 Photographic Reconnaissance Unit at Benson, Oxfordshire. He flew Spitfires which were unarmed to be as light as possible and therefore able to fly at greater heights. In September 1941, just after Kiev had fallen to the Nazis and the Germans had cut off the Crimean Peninsula from the rest of the USSR, Peter was posted missing. We were distraught and CST was in a dreadful state. The tragedy was more than he could bear. His grief was agonising. We walked on the Leas. He was stricken.

"Do you think he's dead?" he asked.

All I could say was, "Yes."

However, nothing, not the war, not his grief over Peter, nothing interfered with his routine of weekdays in London, weekends at Folkestone.

I was in the RAF hospital at Yatesbury to be operated on for a most distressing complaint which unfortunately elicits more sniggers than sympathy from those who have not suffered it – piles. The marvellous attitude of the Welsh sister in charge, who in a very heavy accent would declare, "This is the smartest ward in the hospital" and putting a screen around my bed give me a secret and contraband egg, did little to alleviate the pain. But something else did. As I was Peter's next of kin and also serving in the RAF, a corporal appeared at the end of my bed – he informed me that Peter was safe and was a prisoner of war. On a photographic mission to Hamburg, the engine having failed he had crash-landed near Arnhem in Holland and been captured. I immediately phoned my mother who was overjoyed with the news. Then I phoned the Junior Carlton Club to tell my father. He was not available. After subsequent calls I grew more and more anxious. I should have known I would not find him easily. A few months before Peter had told me of a conversation he had had with a fellow RAF officer who told him he lived at the JC Club.

"Oh," Peter told him, "then you must know my father."

"Why should I?"

"He lives at the club."

"I don't think so. There are only six of us. I don't know your father."

But at the time we took little notice.

When discharged from hospital I took the first train to London. CST was not at his office. I went to the club – the porter was very circumspect.

"Mr Tomlinson is often here around tea-time, Sir," he told me.

I was very angry by the time my father appeared. Even his relief at the news that Peter was safe could not mask his sheepish reaction to my telling him that he did not live where he had for all those years claimed he lived.

"Of course I do, dear boy," he said. "The porter's a bloody fool."

"Now, listen!" The fear I had harboured of this man all the years of my youth vanished. "Please don't pretend that you live at the club. The porter is not a bloody fool and you could have known for days that Peter was safe."

CST was no longer an awesome figure.

"What you do with your life," I told him, "is your own affair. But I must be able to reach you in an emergency."

He simply nodded.

By the weekend he had returned to Folkestone and re-covered his equanimity. He was back again on the same rails. He lived at the club.

In February 1942, Sir Arthur Harris became head of RAF Bomber Command at High Wycombe. He was devoted to Peter and as a tribute to him my younger brother Paul was appointed his personal assistant. Paul had miraculously sur-vived after engine failure had caused his Beaufighter to crash and catch fire immediately after take-off at Wellingore in Lincolnshire. My brother Michael had also briefly filled the post of PA. Michael sailed for Singapore in the troopship *Empire Pride*, but before he arrived the city had fallen to the Japanese and he finished up in Ceylon which would prove to be his home for the next twenty-seven years. I, however, headed in a westerly direction. At last I had been selected for flying training and was on my way to Canada – by way of Manchester. I had to make my way to a transit station lo-cated at Heaton Park. It turned out to be a strange Victorian mansion built by a rich industrialist in large grounds. I ar-rived in Manchester in AC-2s uniform with a groundsheet and full pack on my back. A white flash in my cap indicated that I was an air crew trainee. It was very early in the morning and rain was pouring down. I had no idea where I was or indeed where I was going except that I was supposed to rest up at the YMCA before continuing. I asked a railway porter the way.

"Come on, lad," he said.

Together we exited into the driving rain and he walked me all the way to the YMCA which stood as it still does, next to the Midland Hotel.

"There you are, lad," he said.

I thanked him. He turned and walked off.

"Where are you going?" I asked.

"Back to the station," he replied, dripping wet.

Ever since, I have felt a deep affection for Manchester and for the sort of people who can take that kind of time and trouble for a lost airman.

After Heaton Park I was soon at sea on *The Andes*, a boat which had been built for pleasure cruising the South Atlantic and proved totally unsuitable for its present function. It rolled appallingly. There were those of us going to Canada for training but some of the ship was taken up with German prisoners of war. It seemed to the powers that be a good idea at the time. Would the Germans torpedo a boat that might be full of their own men? They were mostly officers of the Luftwaffe, splendid young Germans. Some of the ship's crew took to shouting obscenities at them while they took their limited exercise, walking up and down a wired-off stretch of deck. They were to spend the rest of the war in POW camps in Canada. I was off to become a trained flyer. For them the war was over but for me it was just beginning.

CHAPTER FIVE

*The tragedies
of war...*

We disembarked at Moncton, a town on the Northumberland Strait, that sliver of the Gulf of St Lawrence which separates Prince Edward Island from New Brunswick. We were soon to be transported by luxury train across the provinces of Quebec and Ontario and round the Great Lakes to Saskatchewan. It was a wonderful journey – quite unforgettable. There, I was first stationed at Assiniboia. The nearest cities had very evocative names – Moose Jaw and Maple Creek. Assiniboia itself seemed the prototypical one-horse town. There was one main street and if the cars had been exchanged for horses they could have shot a cowboy film the authenticity of which would have made John Ford proud. However, down that main street, naturally enough, was that wonderful invention of the New World – the drugstore. There at the dining counter was the kind of food of which one only dreamed back home in those days. I sat at the drugstore counter and enjoyed the huge platter of bacon and eggs. The girl behind the counter was a bit surprised by the strange accent. She regarded me quizzically.

"Where you from?" she asked.

"London," I replied.

"London – Ontario?"

"No, London, England."

She looked at me. She was not about to be taken in.

"O.K. Smarty Pants. You want some more coffee?"

*   *   *

Assiniboia was where I did my elementary flying training. I found myself in a Cornell, a single engine monoplane, preparing to solo. This was always a big moment for every would-be pilot in training and by the time a trainee got the nod from his instructor he was itching to be given the go-ahead. I was no exception and as I was the only pupil on the course with a flying licence I was likely to be the first to solo.

The initial solo involves a circuit and landing of the aerodrome. This consists of taking off into the wind and, at about six hundred feet after levelling off, doing a ninety-degree crosswind turn to port, shortly turning again to port which brings the aircraft flying downwind, i.e. in the opposite direction from take-off. At the right point after two more identical turns the aircraft is in a position to land into the wind onto the runway.

My time had come and I was delighted. My instructor, Sergeant Rathbone, got out of the aircraft and told me what I longed to hear.

"Off you go," said Sgt Rathbone, having made his safety straps safe so that they could not entangle with the control column in his cockpit thereby interfering with mine.

It was an even tougher winter than usual in Canada that year. The snow was deep and the temperature fierce and bitter.

I took off and did all the right things but on the downwind leg of my circuit I was stunned and horrified. The engine had cut out and the propeller was stock-still in front of me. By instinct I turned into wind and from then on luck was on my side. By good fortune I missed some telegraph wires and went between them and the ground. More luck allowed me to pancake the aircraft into deep snow. The aeroplane was quite undamaged.

Although I was in sight of the control tower it took the blood wagon an hour and a half to reach the aircraft and me. It seemed longer than ninety minutes as there was no cabin heat. I had switched everything off.

When they finally arrived the mechanics confirmed that

the aircraft was undamaged and discovered that the engine failure was due to an air-lock in the fuel system. Subsequently my instructor flew the aircraft out after a tractor had cleared the snow to make a reasonable runway for take-off.

I was returned to base on the blood wagon and immediately found myself before the CO. He seemed pleased with me. Aircraft were in short supply.

He took me to the tarmac and pointed at another Cornell.

"Off you go, circuit and landing," he said.

I was delighted and he was still there when I returned having done just that.

"Well done," he said – and that was the end of an eventful day. For a very short time I was Assiniboia's hero.

It is true to say that it is very rare indeed for a training plane to develop engine trouble. Why it should happen to me is anybody's guess.

In Canada we were all British together, those training and those being trained. I didn't see as much of the country as I would have liked at first because I had to work very hard at the theoretical part of the flying training. Book work never came easily to me; having been a total dunce at school, my determination to pass was profound. I never went out at weekends to sample the local delights. I swotted. Luckily, perseverance was rewarded. I passed the course and was sent on to Weyburn for further training. There we flew Harvards. At the end of the course I got my wings and was commissioned as a pilot officer and put in charge of twenty-seven sergeant pilots.

It would have been reward enough for my six months of diligence to get my wings but there was more. We were chosen to do a goodwill tour of Canada. The first stop was Winnipeg where we were greeted as heroes – everything was done to make us comfortable. Bands played and twenty-eight pretty girls were produced to escort us. They took us, individually, home with them where their mothers put on a vast spread. They were wonderfully welcoming and did their best to make us feel part of the family. They usually succeeded. Next came Toronto and the same again – twenty-eight girls and twenty-eight family meals. Then Montreal. We made our way eastward back to Moncton feted at every stop. Canadian hospitality was overwhelming for some of my charges let loose after hard training. At each port of call I lost some. With trepidation I (and my depleted contingent) arrived at Moncton. I went to report to the adjutant. What, I wondered, would be my fate? Cashiered at least.

"Oh hello," he said. "Where you from?"

"Weyburn," my voice was low.

"Jolly good. How many chaps have you got with you?"

I tried evasion. "Well, actually . . ." It was no good. Anyone could count. "They're not all here," I admitted.

"Oh well, they'll turn up. Happens all the time on these goodwill tours. Transport home's not ready yet anyway."

After a week or so hanging around Moncton waiting, I got to know the adjutant in the Mess.

"How would you like to go to New York?" he asked me one day.

I couldn't believe it. But I departed before he changed his mind, with the instruction to ring in every Monday.

"No point in sitting on your arse," he said. "Never know when transport will be available and you're down the list."

In my RAF uniform, the precious wings on my chest, I arrived in New York, perfect casting for the flying hero and was treated as such. I must admit I did nothing to discourage the treatment. I saw Gary Cooper in *For Whom the Bell Tolls* which had just opened at the cinema. Helen Hayes was playing *Harriet* and Ralph Bellamy and Shirley Booth were at the Ethel Barrymore Theatre in *Tomorrow the World*. I saw Alfred Drake and Celeste Holm in *Oklahoma* which was wonderful and Ethel Merman in *Something For the Boys*. Unfortunately I found little for me in the latter. The bellowings of Miss Merman shouting "Hey, Good Looking" were not to my taste, but I am aware that I am in the minority.

It was however all rather dreamlike. Strangers would stop me on Fifth Avenue. It was my first experience of how charming Americans are.

"I just want to say you're doing a great job," they would say patting me on the back and often wanting to take me home with them.

I had arrived not knowing a soul, with only a couple of phone numbers. Within days it seemed I knew the entire city. Invitations poured in. It was in a flat at Sutton Place that I met the most beautiful woman I had ever seen. She was the young widowed mother of two small boys. Her husband, in the 14th/20th Hussars, had been killed in command of a tank in the North African campaign. She was not only beautiful but witty and vivacious as so often American women can be. Although in a way quiet and gentle, she drew everyone to her, becoming the focus of any gathering. She was a talented sculptress as well and in a simple, understated way she always looked quite wonderful. I was surrounded by vital enthusiastic people bursting with energy and always in such company Mary shone. She had travelled widely – been absolutely everywhere. I was dazzled. I lost all regard for practicalities and a whirlwind romance ensued, culminating in a trip to the Justice of the Peace and a September wedding. Some friends lent us a tower flat with a spectacular view of Manhattan. We were so completely in love and taken with each other. It was just too good to be true.

Inevitably, one Monday when I rang Moncton I was told to return. Transport would soon be available. Mary came with me on a wonderful train journey to Canada – but then everything was wonderful with Mary. We had a few more days together in Moncton before I sailed on the *Aquitania* back to England. The ship was full of British airmen who had trained in Canada and the States. We were going back to war. Mary was soon to follow me, once we had overcome the red tape . . . which was to prove more binding than we anticipated.

Harrogate was the centre where assignments were made,

and my first stop. I waited wondering whether I would be flying bombers or fighters and was not terribly pleased with the announcement. Like everyone else, I was keen for operations but instead I was off to Woodley, near Reading, for Flying Instructor's training. I was to teach not perform.

Mainly I was concerned with the arrangements for bringing Mary to England when that dreamlike summer in New York turned into a winter nightmare. Tremendous obstacles stood in the way of my wife joining me. One December weekend I was in London staying with Air Vice-Marshal Graham and his wife Nancy. My youngest brother Paul had married their daughter Anne the previous year. Paul was still PA to Bomber Harris and remained so right through the war, eventually being posted to Headquarters, Combined Operations at Whitehall. We were all working desperately on getting clearance for Mary to join me. There was not a string I was willing to leave unpulled.

Nancy came into my room. "Your father is at his office," she said. "You had better go and see him. He has news for you." Nancy's face could not conceal bad news.

What could have happened? Was it my mother, I wondered. Or Peter? He was still in a prisoner of war camp. I couldn't have begun to imagine the magnitude of the tragedy as I made my confused way to New Bond Street. When I got to the office my mother was there, as well as CST and Paul.

"I've heard from Mary's father," CST told me.

There was no gentle way of telling me. Mary had checked into the Henry Hudson Hotel in New York and from a sixth-floor window had thrown herself and her sons.

The end was as unreal as the romance. There were only questions now to be pondered in my devastation. Why? Could I have done anything to prevent it? The shock and grief were overpowering. My wonderful marriage had such a gruesome ending. Three months – three months spent mainly apart and then nothing except the memories of that laughing, talented girl and the days in the flat with the spectacular views and such happiness as I had never known.

Much later a friend came specially from New York to tell me that Mary had a history of mental illness and the final leap had not been her first attempt at suicide. Somehow that still did not answer my questions. On her grave was placed a statue of a madonna and child which she had sculpted. I have never been able to bring myself to visit it.

That winter I seemed to be surrounded by death. Transferred to Booker airfield near High Wycombe I trained young army NCOs destined for the Rhine crossing, Arnhem and, if need be, Japan. Everything had to be done quickly and their training was very brief. They were taught to sit in a glider – a Hauser or Hengist, great huge craft used for transporting troops, ammunition and supplies. We gave them only three hours' solo flying training. The gliders were towed and they were simply taught to pull the plug, releasing the tow rope and then put the nose down. They could never be sure where they were going to land and no one put a lot of faith in their chances. But this was war and expediency was the order of the day. In actual flying training if a pupil didn't solo after nine to ten hours' dual instruction that was it – CT (cease training) was his fate. There was no time to waste. Everyone did his best but the casualties were horrifying.

That winter also proved to be too much for my mother. There was the uncertainty of the war – Peter was still a POW. There was Mary's tragic death – both my parents had looked forward to an American daughter-in-law. All those things coming on top of her unsatisfactory weekend marriage broke her. Days on end alone at Folkestone dreading what news each day would bring resulted in a nervous breakdown. CST was bewildered and not as understanding of mental trouble as he was of physical illness. He simply couldn't understand. She was taken to a Victorian Gothic hospital in Camberwell. The bleak prison-like edifice sent a shiver through me each time when on the road to Folkestone I passed it years after my mother's thankfully brief sojourn there.

I spent the rest of the war at Booker and life there under our charming commanding officer Wing Commander O'Donnell was delightful. Twice I was seconded to a film unit.

The first film was *Journey Together*, a Ministry of Information film, written by Terence Rattigan and directed by John Boulting. This was the first feature-length film (outside the USSR) to be sponsored entirely by a government. It was written, produced, photographed and acted by members of the RAF and was about the training of flying personnel – and American and British co-operation. Only three civilians appeared in it – Ronald Squire, Bessie Love and Edward G. Robinson, who arrived by bomber from the States and took no salary for his role. I was fascinated by Robinson. Here was a tiny little man with a big stomach and a big bottom who played everything – romantic leads, intellectuals and gangsters. He had an enormous sensitivity which was also reflected in his magnificent art collection. He didn't, however, have an easy family life. His wife was manic-depressive and his son also deeply disturbed. Robinson told me of the day he chopped down the front door with a hatchet. But he remained, despite it all, a charmer and a wonderful laconic story-teller.

"There was this old farmer," he told me, "sitting in a rocking chair out on the porch on a Saturday night with his wife, watching the sun going down over the prairie.

"'You know what, Martha?' he said chewing his pipe and rocking gently.

"'What, George?'

"'Everything's great.'

"'That's right, George.'

"'Cattle are doin' great.'

"'That's right, George.'

"'Wheat's in the barn.'

"'That's right, George.'

"'Everything is fine and dandy.'

"'Fine and dandy, George.'

"'You know Martha but for one thing I'd be a very happy man.'

"'What's that, George?'"

Robinson then left a very lengthy pause.

"'When I think of our daughters laying out there in the graveyard: sometimes I wish they were dead.'"

The actor and writer Arthur McCrae was also filming in *Journey Together* at Pinewood Studios and he knew I needed a flat.

"I saw a board up on Brook Street," he told me one day.

I hurried along as soon as I could and it was marvellous, within walking distance of any London theatre. There was a sitting-room, two bedrooms, a kitchen and bathroom on the top floor across from the Orchid Room nightclub and all for £130 a year. I would have a base for when the war was over – and it was now evident that the end had to be close.

The other film I made while still in uniform was *The Way to the Stars*. Once again I was directed by Anthony Asquith. It was the story of an RAF bomber station and about the co-operation between British and American forces in Britain. Even before the filming started we all realised thankfully that the war would be over before it was shown. Terence Rattigan, who wrote the screenplay, decided to begin the picture with a shot of a bare and derelict airfield. A voice on the soundtrack announced, "This *was* an airfield."

The Way to the Stars was Asquith's greatest and most successful war film – and not a shot was seen to be fired. Edgar Anstey reported in *The Spectator*:

The film acquires nostalgic overtones from a skilled repetition of thought and scene and by the judicious employment of poetry by John Pudney. But most memorable is Anthony Asquith's creation of a typical British and American flying man.

It was a deeply moving film about the death of young men

and more moving, as Dilys Powell pointed out, because there was not a single combat scene in it. There was, however, a good deal of flying.

"I wish the planes would fly closer together," Asquith said. "Why are they so far apart?"

"That," he was told, "would be rather dangerous."

"It can't be dangerous," he persisted, "if they're not actually touching."

Perhaps he was not technologically astute but Asquith was emotionally sensitive and could be moved to tears.

"Floods," as he called it – "Oh my dear, floods."

He remained as eccentric as ever. Although no one ever knew what his duties were he was in the Home Guard and dressed always in uniform and heavy boots.

After four years Peter was finally liberated at Lübeck while on a march to Flensburg. He had spent the war in camps in Frankfurt-am-Main, Warburg, Schubin in Poland and finally Bremen. He landed at Wing Aerodrome in Buckinghamshire and rang Bomber Command. He was immediately put through to Air Chief Marshal Sir Arthur Harris.

"Where are you?" Harris asked.

"I'm at High Wycombe station."

"Wait there," he was told, and Harris soon arrived to fetch him. He was in a hurry. He always was and wasn't averse to driving his works Bentley up on the pavements and through traffic lights.

Peter was thin as a rake after four years in camps and the final horrendous march under the guard of the SS. The Chief of the RAF Bomber Command Air Chief Marshal Sir Arthur Harris personally took charge of his recuperation.

"Peter," he said, "anything of mine is yours – up to half my kingdom."

CST hurried to see his favourite son. He was overjoyed to see him. There was a quick embrace and then holding Peter at arm's length, his first words to his son were: "Old boy – have you got any petrol coupons?"

CHAPTER SIX

*In which
I sign a
movie contract
and discover
good friends...*

In 1946 I was demobilised. For the last six months before my release I had spent most of my time going up to London on a motorbike which I bought for seven pounds and ten shillings. There was the Brook Street flat to get organised. Then, after the end of that interruption to real life called the Second World War, I sold the bike, recouping my original investment exactly.

In the cinema that year the war was still being dissected. In *I See a Dark Stranger* Deborah Kerr played an Irish maid who so hated the English she collaborated with the Nazis. I played an Intelligence Officer. After that I was a young scientist who gets killed in an experimental flight in *School for Secrets* – the story of the development of radar. It was Peter Ustinov's first attempt at directing a feature film.

"You haven't met Ralph Richardson, have you?" Peter asked and he called the great man over.

Ralph came over to us. "Hello," he said simply and succinctly and then did a circular detour around the room rather like a principal boy in a pantomime. He was deep in thought. His hat was perched on the side of his head. He came back, looked me in the eye and said, "Chilly, isn't it."

Off he went again around the room.

I looked at Peter who just smiled.

Ralph was certainly an eccentric actor in an irresistible way. It was impossible to take your eyes off him – on stage, on screen or indeed when he was doing one of his wandering promenades around a room. Probably his eccentricity was a defence mechanism because when we sat down to talk it was a completely different story.

We had quite a few scenes together on our own and we lunched together.

"Hear you had a nasty time, cocky," he said to me one day.

I wondered what he meant.

"Your wife, dear boy."

Mary's suicide had been headlines in the New York newspapers and had indeed been reported in a more discreet way in England. Ralph was himself no stranger to tragedy. By the time we met he had been happily married to the actress Meriel Forbes for two years but an earlier marriage probably still haunted him. He was only twenty-two and Muriel (Kit – short for Kitten) Hewitt was seventeen when they had married in 1924. He had been besotted by her beauty and natural grace and rated her acting talent far above his own. In those youthful days so did many others, but Ralph had no jealousy, only admiration and deep love. Within four years Kit contracted a bizarre and devastating virus – encephalitis lethargica – a sleeping sickness but a particularly tragic kind of sleeping sickness. It affected the brain and the body equally, making movement difficult and uncontrollable as well as producing the fluctuating emotions of mania and depression. For fourteen years Kit lived in a topsy-turvy world, sometimes as a zombie and at other times in great pain. She was looked after by dear friends but Ralph was never far away, always hurrying to visit her on his great Harley Davidson motorcycle. No matter where he had been performing, he hurried to Kit's side whenever possible. He was carving out his career and was desolate that they could no longer share a stage. She bore her illness with great fortitude but the constant awareness they shared that there was no hope of recovery and that the pain and lack of physical and mental control would only increase was a great burden.

Kit was found dead one morning, suffocated in her bed. A

knotted scarf was wound round her neck and caught in the bedpost. Life had become too much for her to bear any longer. The coroner's verdict was a kind one – misadventure. Ralph was never sure whether or not Kit's death had been an accident, but like me, when I thought about Mary, he wondered if there was anything he could have done which would have prevented the tragedy. His sympathy for me was enormously comforting and I have never forgotten his kindness.

At the end of the war my brother Peter, after an extended goodwill tour of Scandinavia and the United States, had settled in South Africa where he was freight manager of the Safmarine Shipping Company which was founded by Sir Arthur "Bomber" Harris. Michael decided to stay in Ceylon where he followed our maternal ancestors into the tea-planting business. He learned to speak Singhalese and Tamil and loved the island. Paul moved to the United States where he became an insurance adjustor. He soon moved on to the china business, first with Josiah Wedgwood in New York and then with the Royal Worcester Porcelain Company of which he became President in Toronto until his retirement.

It was not easy furnishing my flat in Brook Street in the aftermath of the war when in England rationing remained. For years I had longed for a place of my own where I could put into effect all the ideas I had about interior design. Because of rationing I had to modify some of my ideas but luckily you didn't need coupons for period Regency and Victorian furniture.

I adored the flat. It was very close to the Mayor Gallery and I used to walk the hundred yards and spend hours chatting to Freddy Mayor. He was a very funny man. In his younger days, he told me, he had been rather wild – much taken to attending all-night parties.

"I do wish," his mother told him, "you wouldn't go to those parties where people blow smoke in your face."

He found it highly amusing and rather touching that his mother never for a moment thought that her son might be a culprit rather than a victim.

By the time I knew him he was happily married to charming Pammy, the wild nights a memory and source of amusing tales. He was the most respected and honest art dealer, with a marvellous eye. He specialised in the Impressionists and I took to them immediately myself. He sold me a Bonnard landscape which I loved. It was a beautiful picture. I hated parting with it but I couldn't resist selling it back to him a few years later for ten times the price I paid him. His son is now a specialist in Very Modern painting – a taste I cannot share.

Downstairs from me in Brook Street lived an elderly lady. She lived alone except for her maid, but I was aware that she entertained a number of gentleman callers. One day the cockney commissionaire of the nightclub across the road said to me, "What about the one underneath you?"

I was rather evasive and said, "I don't know what you mean."

"The whore under you," he said knowingly. "She must be nigh on seventy. I don't know how she does it – never short of punters." He paused for thought. "She must have a tricky finish."

One day soon after that she stopped me on the stairs and gently handed me a newspaper.

"Please look," she said proudly.

There in the paper was a marriage announcement. The lady had married a bank manager.

"I'm a good girl now," she announced with a proud smile. As far as I was concerned she was a good girl and a good neighbour and I wished her well.

A much more important lady came into my life during the Brook Street days. I was at Brenda Bruce's flat extolling the virtues of *my* flat when her housekeeper said, "You'll need some help then. I have a friend."

Alice arrived the next morning on a bus from Battersea, brought me breakfast on a tray and she and her husband Ernie have been around my family ever since, a constant source of help and occasionally a source of interesting information.

"Did I ever tell you about the time I saw a tram accident on Lavender Hill?" she once asked.

"No, I don't think you ever did."

"Well, a woman was waiting with her daughter to get off the tram. The daughter thought there was something wrong and wisely jumped off. In fact the tram had come off its tracks and fell onto its side. All the passengers were trapped and the mother of the girl eventually lost both her legs – up to her knees. They picked them up and put them on the pavement."

"Alice – you made it up."

"No, I didn't – I saw it."

I soon learned to rely on Alice and to trust her completely. Never had I met anybody more intelligent. Once I rang Alice from abroad and she negotiated a film contract for me. She can cope with anything which is just as well because I've never had an agent. I didn't want anyone dealing with my affairs who was also dealing with seventy other actors – or seventeen or even seven for that matter. I've never understood why actors seem to be frightened of negotiation. It depends on two things only. Do they want you and can they pay?

The conversation always begins the same way. The producer starts off saying he has no money. In more than fifty years in the business I have never known a producer (except Disney) who admits to having money.

"I'm sorry you have no money," I then say, "but this is what I am paid." Then I name a sum, which is what they probably know I was last paid.

This evokes a sharp intake of breath from him. "I don't think we can pay that," is the invariable reply.

It is of course important to know the going rate for the job and also never to lie or bluff. That is the producer's prerogative. "I'm sure," I then continue, "there are a lot of people who will do it for less and I only hope that one day you will be richer or I'll be poorer and then perhaps we can work together."

I've never lost a job through negotiation. My first big deal was with the Rank organisation. David Healey asked me to meet him at Rank's South Street office, a stone's throw from my flat.

"Would you like to be a contract player?" he asked.

"Yes, please," I said without hesitation and that was that. They were good employers and it was an excellent contract, though I must say not as good as Eric Portman's. He was being paid by Rank virtually until his death. But I happily joined the stars.

Rank was very keen on publicity. Birthdays were celebrated in style for the benefit of the press. Stunts were organised. Romances mooted. There were endless parties and photo sessions but I didn't get too involved in that. However, I did agree to one that I thought unusually clever and great fun. I took Valerie Hobson up in a plane and a camera was fixed above my head to photograph her. It made a good spread in *Picture Post*. Mostly, though, I worked from one picture to the next with barely a break.

The most interesting of the lot was *Miranda*. This was a fantasy about a mermaid who tricks a Harley Street doctor into taking her home with him so that she can see the sights of London. Tail wrapped in a blanket and ensconced in a wheelchair she gets her way. Like all mermaids, she is very manipulative and a siren. Soon all the males in the film fall under her spell and are at her beck and call, protesting undying love and proposing marriage. The doctor's wife gets wise to her and sends Miranda back to the sea with the true definition of a mermaid ringing in her ears – sea cow.

I was not originally cast in the film. But after three weeks of shooting the first version was scrapped and re-cast. I was given the part of Charles the enamoured chauffeur. It was a good part and the first time the critics began referring to my "sadly heroic face". The truth is that I may look like a disappointed spaniel but by nature I am cheerful – honestly.

Glynis Johns played Miranda and had grown up since she knitted me a sweater during the run of *Quiet Wedding*. She was now twenty-three. I spent a good deal of the film carrying her around and will never again believe there is any such thing as a light lady. I discounted at once all those Hollywood scenes of eager young husbands carrying their brides over the threshold. It was extremely hard work carrying Glynis around. Of course the tail (by Dunlop) might have made it more difficult.

CHAPTER SEVEN

*Encountering
Robert Morley,
Errol Flynn
and the
beloved Audrey...*

B inkie Beaumont rang me up one day and said, "How would you like to play a leading part in a brilliant play?"

I said, "Yes, please."

The play was *The Little Hut* and in its original French by André Roussin, it had been a great Parisian success. Noël Coward had done an adaptation and so had Emlyn Williams but the clever Binkie believed neither was exactly right and in the end Binkie gave it to Nancy Mitford. She understood the problems immediately and wrote to her mother:

It's a terribly funny play about husband, lover and wife on a desert island – lover gets very low all alone in the little hut while husband and wife sleep in the big one, insists on taking turns. Husband not absolutely delighted but sees the logic, that they have shared her for six years and might as well go on doing so. Then a handsome young negro appears, ties up husband and lover by a trick and indicates that he will only let them go if Susan will go into the hut with him, which she is only too pleased to do as he is very good looking. "Disgusting" I hear you say. And so on – you see the form. It is terribly funny, *I* think but I never counted on it much as everyone says the Lord Chamberlain wouldn't pass it. Here [Paris] it has run over three years, a wild success. I've skated over the worst indecencies, in fact the reason I was asked to do it was that I'm supposed to be good at making outrageous situations seem all right. Roussin, the author, an utter love, doesn't know a word of English so I've got away with altering it a great deal.

This was Nancy Mitford's first and last excursion into theatrical writing. It was not an experience she actually enjoyed very much, being used to an aristocratic, if eccentric, lifestyle. She preferred dining at eight rather than sitting in the theatre stalls taking notes and preparing to re-write scenes. Moreover, she was still of the opinion that actors were vagabonds and gypsies and not quite "people one knew". She did, however, produce the goods, then firmly refused to dip her toe into theatrical waters ever again. She certainly didn't sink in them but found constantly swimming against the tide of her inclinations an unnecessary exertion for a distinguished novelist and eventually as distinguished an historian.

Having got the script, Binkie cast Robert Morley and me, not two actors noted for sexiness, as the husband and lover. Joan Tetzel, a beautiful American actress, who was married to Oscar Homolka, was the wife. There could be nothing even faintly tasteless about Joan, who was the epitome of chic.

For the set, Binkie got the most sought-after theatrical designer of the time – and indeed of most times – Oliver Messel, who created for the play one of his most memorable sets. The desert island was a breathtaking fantasy. There were huge overblown flowers and breadfruit that could be seen ripening before the eyes of the audience. And as a final stylish touch, Balmain was commissioned to design Joan's frock.

The 25-year-old *enfant terrible*, Peter Brook, who had made his London début aged eighteen at the Torch Theatre with a production of *Dr Faustus* and subsequently had great success with a number of productions of Shakespeare, Shaw and indeed *Boris Godunov* at Covent Garden, was engaged to direct. He had worked earlier that year with Messel on the

Anouilh/Fry *Ring Around the Moon* and had another notable success. He was meticulous in translating Messel's model set to the stage. Brook pointed out to him in a letter, while we were on the pre-London tour in Glasgow,

> whether your success is maintained in this or not depends solely on how exquisitely you get your craftsmen to put their finishing touches. The least tattiness or lack of finish and the whole show is down the drain.

It has to be said that there were not just three principal characters in *The Little Hut*: the set was a fourth.

My first meeting with Robert Morley, who had established himself as a West End star fifteen years before in *Oscar Wilde* and consolidated his success with *The Man Who Came to Dinner*, *The First Gentleman*, and the marvellous *Edward, My Son* (which he also wrote), was on stage. This was my first West End part (if you don't count carrying a crown on a pillow in *The Merchant of Venice*). But Robert and I did have something in common – Folkestone. He had grown up there too. We shared common memories of the Leas, Canon Elliott and once we had even shared communal gardens as our respective houses backed out onto them. We were introduced.

"My brother went to school with you," I said, chattily.

He fixed me with a glassy stare, shot his cuffs, turned his back and walked away from me.

Well, that's a good start, I thought, and worried about the imminent future during which we would have to work together very closely indeed. I soon learned never, never, never to mention school to Robert. It is a fatal topic of discussion as he loathed it even more deeply than I did. That was something I would never have thought possible. Our relationship, luckily, improved.

Peter Brook, however, continued to have a difficult time. He was not, in our view, an attractive man – and good heavens, wasn't he young. Robert fought him every step of the way. Brook felt that the foreign element of the play should be intensified for English audiences. Furthermore he seemed to enjoy rehearsals for their own sake. Robert hated rehearsing. He wanted an audience. On the first day of rehearsal he said to me, "Here we are on a bare stage with one light bulb hanging from the flies and you look around at the other actors and think how can it be possible that in four weeks' time an audience is going to be prepared to pay to see us?" It is true that one can get very sick of rehearsals. All through that period you feel something is missing – something vital. Then on the first night you find it – the audience.

Brook, in spite of Robert, by sheer tenacity held the production in his hands . . . well, more or less, and with a good deal of help from Binkie. Brook didn't direct Robert and swiftly learned that that was not a part of his brief. Robert was simply impossible to control. I realised when watching him at close and not so close quarters that he was determined to give the audience what he thought they wanted: BIMBO THE CLOWN – HERE WE ARE AGAIN, is how I would describe it.

When we began rehearsals I couldn't believe that Robert planned to do what he was doing "on the night", but he did and the audience loved it. So ultimately did I. The audience reaction to him was equal to the response elicited by Max Miller. In my book there could be nothing better than that.

For my part, I learned to try to keep up with him. I also could juggle – all kinds of things. I juggled coconuts, fishing rods and grapes. We did a tour of the provinces, Nancy constantly re-writing, Oliver Messel tinkering with the set and Peter Brook pulling his hair out. Then, on Wednesday August 23rd, 1950, we opened at the Lyric Theatre on Shaftesbury Avenue. The critic John Gay reported that he "was embarrassed and so were many people around me. Maybe the censor needs a new pair of glasses."

The *Sunday Chronicle* was apoplectic. "In the third act immorality is capped by snobbishness and the curtain falls on downright vulgarity."

Luckily other critics found it "delightful", "absurd", "one

of the gayest things in London theatreland". I don't keep reviews as a rule but I treasure one from the *New York Times* by Moss Hart.

> Robert Morley, astonishingly enough, turns out to be a first rate farceur, and though the part of the cuckolded husband is one that he could certainly play in his sleep (which is what he seemed to be doing the night we saw him) he is nevertheless enormously funny. Again, surprisingly enough, Miss Joan Tetzel, a rather mannered young actress, is quite engaging as the wife, but the most enjoyable performance of the piece, it seemed to me, is given by David Tomlinson. He plays the lover in a paroxysm of petulance that is little short of hilarious and turns a part that could quickly descend into dullness into a minor thespian miracle.

I accept "minor" and treasure it because it gave me the edge over Robert for a change and we did become very competitive on stage and off as we settled into a long run – just how long I couldn't have imagined on that first night.

During the run of *The Little Hut* I changed London flats, bought a house in the country and got married. I also made eight films and learned to cope with Robert Morley on stage. His love of tinkering with a play during rehearsals is only exceeded by his love of tinkering with the production in front of an audience. You have to be on your toes to keep up with Morley, as one night I was, literally, for the entire first act. Imagine the scene. The curtain goes up and I'm on stage with Joan Tetzel. There I am, immaculate in evening dress on this magnificent desert island set – but I have only one shoe on. At Robert's entrance he is meant to toss me the other shoe saying, "You can have that, Henry."

Then I continue the scene fully shod. Joan used to negotiate the way backstage from her dressing-room to the wings in an old pair of beaded slippers, mules, I believe they are called, which she changed for extremely high heels before making her entrance. When she came off the stage she left the shoes in the wings and put the slippers back on. That night Robert came on, her tiny slipper dangling from his enormous barge-like foot.

"Here," he says, throwing the tiny shoe to me, "you can have that."

I was determined that Robert was not going to break me up. There is a school of critics which very much disapproves of onstage shenanigans but here I plead an excuse. The object of the play is to keep the audience amused and in a long run, if the actors are bored so is the audience. I played the whole scene curiously shod as if it were the most natural thing in the world – and tears of suppressed laughter rolled down Robert's cheeks. He was delighted.

That, however, was a minor incident compared to the enormous mental anguish he later inflicted on me. There was, in the play, one exchange that went thus:

"What about Dotty? Did she have a lover?"

"Of course. She went to Paris with him at Easter."

"I thought she was in a party of seven."

"Well, the other five dropped out."

We regularly used this conversation to relieve the boredom, inserting another name, usually a friend who was out front. One night some South African acquaintances were in the audience. They were called Stuttaford and owned a department store in Cape Town where they knew my brother, Peter:

"What about Mrs Stuttaford?" I asked. "Did she have a lover?"

The exchange then continued as written. At the interval a messenger arrived at my dressing-room delivering a hand-written note.

"I don't know if the mention of my wife's name was meant as a joke," I read, "but without prejudicing any further action I may see fit to take in this matter, I wish you to know that it was in the worst possible taste and we shall certainly not be dining with you after the show."

My blood ran cold. After all, I didn't know the Stuttafords

very well. I had made a terrible mistake. Was it libel or slander for which I was about to be sued? Should I ring my father immediately so he could recommend a good barrister? Instead I hurried down to consult the stage manager, dear Mary Lynn. There at the side of the stage sat Robert eating a huge bar of Cadbury's chocolate. It seemed that he hadn't even bothered to remove the silver paper.

"Mary," I asked the stage manager, "where did this note come from? Do you think they'll sue?"

Robert took it from me, read it and handed it back saying, "I don't think so. Mind you, you have to be so careful with the colonials."

I spent the rest of the play in an emotional sweat imagining the four beady eyes of the Stuttafords fixed on me as they planned to contact their solicitor. After the curtain fell the knock came on the dressing-room door. I froze. In came the South Africans brandishing not writs but compliments. They were full of cheer.

"Delightful evening, couldn't have enjoyed it more."

Eventually I twigged. Robert had got his dresser to write the note.

The run was full of incident – and not all of it of Robert's making. Roger Moore was my second understudy and first to the savage played by Geoffrey Toone. Roger had fallen in love with Dorothy Squires. One evening as I was preparing to leave the theatre he came into my dressing-room scratched and with blood pouring down his face. His wife and her mother had found out about the affair and waited to confront him outside the stage door. I told him to wash his face – it wasn't as bad as it looked – and guided him to safety through the stalls and out of the front door. He was a nice young fellow but he didn't take my advice to stay with his wife. He married Dorothy Squires.

Joan Tetzel was amazing. She invariably stayed in bed until forty-five minutes before the curtain was due to rise. She then took a taxi straight to the theatre. Her make-up took her barely five minutes. Joan always looked impeccable and was never late for her entrance.

The management's PR lady Vivien Brierley was always coming up with bizarre schemes to attract publicity. She would persuade me into unlikely costumes to attract the attention of the press. One day she arranged for a very attractive model to be photographed on the set of *The Little Hut*. It was apropos absolutely nothing, except perhaps a picture in the paper keeping the name of the show in front of the ticket-buying public. The poor girl was speechless in her embarrassment. She had no idea what she was doing there. Her boyfriend arrived to fetch her after the photo session. He was Bill Meldon, an ex-policeman from Dorset who was a rower and an athlete. We struck up a conversation while waiting for the girl to change, and became great friends.

Robert used, very wisely, to avoid getting involved with Miss Brierley's attempts to attract publicity. He did, however, try very hard to get me married off to a charming girl. But luckily we both decided it was not a good idea and not surprisingly she has managed her life very happily ever since without me.

Being in a hit West End show and, it seemed, constantly visible on the cinema screens in 1951, I was asked to appear at the Royal Command Performance. There I was presented to King George VI and Queen Elizabeth. Errol Flynn was also on the bill. He was staying out of the United States a lot at that time for tax purposes and also to avoid huge alimony payments, and had just made a film in France, *The Adventures of Captain Fabia*, with Micheline Presle. He had written the original screenplay himself. But the film unfortunately was not a patch on his early Hollywood hits like *The Adventures of Robin Hood* (the first Technicolor film to be a major success if you don't count *Snow White*) and *The Dawn Patrol*. Those movies made him one of the top ten box-office stars a decade before our meeting. But Flynn's notorious life style was now the focus of attention. He was newly married to his third wife, Patrice Wymore who had just signed a contract with his studio, Warners, that kept her a lot busier than he was being kept by them.

Flynn was notorious for drink and women. He had been cleared in America on two indictments in which it was alleged that he had had unlawful sexual intercourse with under-aged girls – eighteen being the legal age of consent. He was defending a ten-year-old paternity suit and was in general the object of lots and lots of gossip. Still, he maintained a nice line in self-deprecation. He had toured the Alaskan army bases with a concert party after his notorious trial and, some said, rather dubious acquittal. His opening line on that occasion set the tone of the evening.

"There were thousands of people waiting to see me off at the airport," he told the audience. "Most of them were lawyers."

It had been five years since he had made enormous headlines in London but no one had forgotten the uproar over his film *Operation Burma*. It was about American paratroopers in an offensive against the Japanese in Burma during the Second World War. It was shot in a muddy terrain near Los Angeles' Santa Anita race-track. Unfortunately the film neglected to give credit to the British Fourteenth Army in Burma and once more Errol Flynn seemed to win the war single-handed. When it opened in September 1945 at the Warner Cinema in Leicester Square mobs picketed in fury and the film was immediately withdrawn from release.

At the Command Performance Flynn came on with Walter Pidgeon. Pidgeon's films that year were *Soldiers Three* and *Calling Bulldog Drummond* but he had, a couple of years before, made *That Forsyte Woman* (Hollywood's version of *The Forsyte Saga* and one of Flynn's best films) with him. The repartee was scripted.

"How's Burma?" Pidgeon asked.

"I never laid a finger on her," was the reply and of course it brought the house down. I spent some time with him then and later we met up again.

Years later Flynn took to turning up at the Lyric Theatre. The set of *The Little Hut* was open at the side and when I would see him standing in the wings I knew he wanted company for supper. He was a lonely man and we often dined together. He was certainly a drinker, although I never saw him remotely drunk. He was still very good looking and still had an extraordinary effect on women – an effect he didn't seem to understand.

One night he said, "What are you doing this weekend, sport?"

I told him I was driving down to Folkestone to see my mother who was convalescing from one of her many operations.

He thought about it. "I might come with you," he said; and he did.

On the way we stopped for a cup of tea at a roadside café and I have never seen such a reaction as I witnessed from the woman who served us. I thought she would faint away. She just stood there shaking with excitement at the sight of Flynn. And it wasn't just because he was a film star. There was something about the appeal he generated. The poor woman was simply unable to function properly. He was charming with her, but he found it a problem to cope with the response he called forth from women – unintentionally, he assured me.

Needless to say my mother, too, was rendered speechless when he put his head around the bedroom door.

We met often. We talked about the early days in Northampton rep when he played the wicked prince in *Jack and the Beanstalk* and then went on to larger parts in *Yellow Sands* and *The Farmer's Wife*. They were for him among his happiest days. He was always interesting and I decided he was a much maligned character then and of course even more so after his death. The simple truth is that he was a very good actor. Olivier once told me that he believed that if Errol had wanted to he could have been the greatest classical star in the theatre. He had a natural grace and charm that is too often denigrated. He despised being treated as a pawn in the Hollywood game. He resented the fact that little seemed to be done to produce good scripts. It wasn't thought to be necessary. His magnetism was enough. All they had to do was get him in front of the camera and the queues would form at the box office.

"I never wanted to play Hamlet," he said, "but I did want to do something just a little bit better than the crap they've been putting me in." He hated it when his friends came up and said, "Saw your film, Errol – bloody awful wasn't it?" He could only agree and it hurt him deeply. But Flynn never lost his sense of humour. In one of the last interviews he gave before his death in October, 1959 he said, "The rest of my life will be devoted to women and litigation." He was often underrated by those who would not know the difference between a good and a bad film actor. Like Cooper and Leslie Howard, he always made it look easy. I liked him enormously and he was always marvellous company.

About this time I decided that what I really wanted was a country retreat . . . a little cottage away from the hurly-burly of London. I was playing every night and sometimes filming in the day but still there were Sundays when a bit of a garden and greenery would be welcome as well as a bit more space for my growing collection of period furniture and paintings. I used to go down to Buckinghamshire to visit the elderly mother of an antique dealer who was a friend of mine. She lived in a very seductive little village and I loved it.

"If you ever hear of anything going around here do let me know," I told her.

A few weeks later she rang. "There is a bit of land for sale," she informed me.

"I don't want land." I wanted somewhere to live.

"I just thought you would like to know," she added.

"How much land?" I asked.

"I don't know."

"Well, how much do they want for it?"

"I don't know."

It was such a bizarre conversation that I became curious

and went down to look at it. It turned out to be a couple of acres and on the spur of the moment I bought it. There had been a pub there called the Six Lords Inn. That had burned to the ground. Later a house had been built on the plot – that, too, burned down. It was probably just as well that I didn't get planning permission to build there. Perhaps the property was haunted by a pyromaniac spirit.

While I was negotiating over that land I did, however, hear of a derelict cottage in the area, which belonged to Sir Thomas Beecham's son Adrian. It was adjacent to Beecham's rather grand 1890s house, Mursley Hall. The cottage was just rotting away and prospective buyers got nowhere because Beecham simply wasn't interested in dealing with them. He was difficult to contact. But I heard he was interested in the theatre so I got his address and wrote to him and invited him to come and see *The Little Hut*. Adrian was pleased to accept the invitation. He came to the theatre, joined me for supper and sold me the cottage with an acre of land.

Being now a land-owning gentleman, I moved from the flat in Brook Street to a tiny *pied-à-terre* in Chelsea. The flat was tiny – one room with a kitchenette and a bathroom, but the hall of the building was enormous and has lately been done over.

"What do you think of the hall, Alice?" I asked her.

"More front than Brighton," was Alice's reply.

My nest-building instincts were now channelled into the cottage at Mursley. There was plenty of scope for improvement. In fact, even now, some thirty-five years later, I'm still working on it.

I was filming at Pinewood on *Made in Heaven* when I saw the most fetching young redhead. (Later I was to learn it wasn't red, it was titian.) She had come down to see the director of the film on which I was working. Her name, I quickly discovered, was Audrey Freeman, and I thought she was dazzlingly pretty.

She was at the time a principal dancer in *Zip Goes a Million* with four cameo roles and several dance numbers opening the first and second half of the show with spectacular effect. She had been trained as a dancer since her childhood. Her intelligence is her own but her goodness and character result from marvellous parents, the proverbial salt of the earth and the best of England. Their home was and still is in Barnsley, a name that seems to produce merriment when mentioned. It is not a town of much beauty but is surrounded by gorgeous countryside. Audrey was stunning – and also a no-nonsense Yorkshire lass.

That was the beginning. I cooked her eggs in screw-top ramekins (my specialty) and then most nights, as she opened the show at the Palace and her curtain went up before mine at the Lyric I could watch her perform. She greatly admired George Formby, the star of the show, who she told me came to the first rehearsal word perfect. He knew every line – his and everyone else's. I was told not long ago that this was because Formby couldn't read. I suppose this is possible because Audrey said he never consulted a script.

I was lucky enough to marry Audrey on May 17th, 1953 at Ealing Register Office. It was ten days after my thirty-sixth birthday. Audrey was just twenty-one.

"I shan't give up my career," she told me.

"Quite right," I agreed. "I need the money."

The wedding was both quiet and secret although the Rank Organisation managed to get some mileage out of the fact that my latest film was *Is Your Honeymoon Really Necessary?* and the fact that Audrey played the maid in the film – her first and last movie role.

Mary Lynn, the stage manager of *The Little Hut*, was there with her husband. Bill Meldon was my best man and of course dear Alice was with us.

"It was fine first thing," she observed laconically; "it is raining now." She was right, it was.

That was a bit of an understatement, even for Alice. It absolutely poured.

A honeymoon was not only unnecessary – it was impossible. We were both back at work the next day. Audrey by
now was playing a major role in the highly successful musical *Love from Judy* at the Saville Theatre and I was still in *The
Little Hut*.

CHAPTER EIGHT

*In which
I become a father,
survive a plane crash
and become
fascinated by
Peter Sellers...*

I suppose I always pictured myself having a family but after the trauma of my first marriage it seemed a remote possibility until I met Audrey. We moved into the unfurnished cottage at Mursley together. From then it grew with us. It wasn't a case of Audrey moving into my home after the marriage. It was true that I had already bought it, and indeed begun work on it – but it was just a house. It wasn't a home until Audrey crossed the threshold. She planned to have our first child there. It wasn't a good idea. The labour seemed to go on for ever and finally an ambulance was summoned to take her to the Royal Bucks Hospital in Aylesbury. I'll never forget getting into my car and trailing after the ambulance, tears streaming down my face. She'll never forget it either. What a great help I was. I really thought she was going to die. Instead she produced an incredible eight-and-one-half-pound boy, David Redvers – named after her father. It was April 6th, 1954 and at the age of thirty-seven I was a proud parent. Even after the birth when it was obvious that mother and child were doing well, as they say, I was still very shaken. The enormity of having a child was overwhelming.

"You know how sentimental I am," I told her in an attempt to explain my feelings as we drove home from the hospital.

"So was Hitler," she replied. In our thirty-seven years of marriage, her Yorkshire feet have always been firmly planted on the ground.

Miraculously, David had been born on CST's seventy-first birthday. As David was his first male grandchild, we expected particular excitement from him. Rather surprisingly his interest was at best polite and perfunctory. Little did we know then that the advent of a grandson was not quite such an historic event as we thought at the time.

CST continued to persist with his fantasy that he lived at his club during the week. From time to time, I dropped the odd hint that I thought this was patently absurd. No doubt provoked by this, he invited my brothers and me to the club for a drink. We were shown up to a rather drab little bedroom. A couple of hairbrushes lay on a chest of drawers. I resisted the temptation to open the drawers to see if they were empty.

"How about a drink, old boy!" said CST to nobody in particular. We welcomed the idea. The wine waiter was summoned. We told him what we wanted.

"I'll have the usual," said CST, affecting nonchalance.

The waiter disappointed him.

"What is that, Sir?"

The failure of this subterfuge must have appalled my father.

Of course, I reflected on this latest chapter in the mystery but the joy of our first child's arrival took precedence over everything.

Louise, the eldest of the sisters who had looked after us at Folkestone, came down for several weeks to take care of Audrey and little David. After moving on from my family, she had joined the Royal Victoria Hospital where without the benefit of much formal education, she eventually became assistant matron and was for twenty-six years in charge of the children's ward. There was not very much that she did not know about children. A consultant there had once said to me, "We don't tell her. She tells us."

Louise was a very clever, dedicated spinster, quietly, it is said, in unrequited love with a married man all her life. Of course, she was also a dictator. She walked in and took over.

"Off to bed with you. I'll bring you a cup of tea!" she barked at a grateful Audrey, ordering her out of the kitchen on her return from hospital with David.

Audrey put her feet up and was happy to let Louise get on with everything. They were devoted to each other. She was a very remarkable lady and she certainly adored Audrey.

I occupied myself on stage with a domestic comedy and a different nanny. In *All for Mary* the lady of the title takes her second husband (me) on honeymoon to the Alpine resort where she spent her first honeymoon. Naturally, the previous husband turns up. He and I come down with chicken-pox and we are put to bed in the same room. A nurse is summoned, Nannie Cartwright. Kathleen Harrison in that part was the prototype of all bossy nannies. She treated us, two supposedly grown men, as if we were naughty boys.

"Won't," she told us, "that's a little word we *never* use."

Kathleen stole the show, deservedly. As one critic complimenting her faultless timing and inflection wrote: "She so dominates the scene that if the play went on ten minutes longer everyone would be reduced to utter baby talk."

We had opened it in Brighton and it was far from right. It was slight and everything depended on the playing. Henry Sherek presented it and in Brighton, I told him, "We can only get this going if you sit in the stalls and give us your support at rehearsals."

Luckily all was well and not only did it have a long London run but we then toured it and afterwards it was made into a film. The movie version, directed by Wendy Toye, had a number of alterations to the original. Now there was no marriage, no honeymoon. Instead, two Englishmen compete for the love of the Alpine hotelier's French daughter. I played Humpy Miller ("dim and cuddly") and Nigel Patrick played my original role, Clive Norton ("beastly and attractive"). We still got chicken-pox (although some cinema reviewers inexplicably thought it was measles) and luckily Kathleen Harrison still played Nanny Cartwright and stole the film as deservedly as she had the stage play. Kathleen Harrison is a wonderful actress.

David was two and Audrey decided to have another go at the theatre. She was offered the part of principal boy in the Christmas pantomime at Plymouth and eagerly accepted. I was delighted. I love Christmas and I have adored panto-mimes ever since those Folkestone days when I thrilled to the marvellous Murray King's shows. What a wonderful excuse Audrey gave me to go often. I did and took David who enjoyed it as much as I did. Of course I encouraged him and the audience to boo the witch and joined in myself very loudly. The audience responded.

"Give us a chance," the witch admonished me later. "Let me get the lines out."

Audrey was just a few weeks into her second pregnancy when she had costume fittings for the part – but she was fast approaching her fifth month when the show closed and during the run she studiously faced front, avoiding giving the audience even a glimpse of her profile. It was a very happy time and we all enjoyed it greatly, but then Audrey hung up her dancing shoes and retired to the kitchen where occasionally I can persuade her to tap dance or do a time step.

As before, Audrey had a long and difficult labour – we actually expected this. But on June 14th, 1956 she presented me with our second son James Adam, a splendid boy. David was delighted to have a brother. Once again Louise returned to rule the roost.

Jamie was just ten months old when an accident nearly left my young family fatherless.

It was Friday, April 12th, 1957. A distant relation who lived near by was eager to fly so I took him to Luton Aero Club and I hired a Tiger Moth. To keep your pilot's licence active you have to fly so many hours a year. I was therefore quite keen on the flight. Since the war I had done about seventy hours of flying and I still loved it. I have never forgotten when David Llewelyn took me above the clouds. It was a magical experience.

We took off with me in the front cockpit as in my instructor days. My passenger was in the seat behind me. We flew over Mursley and then south-east of the village climbed to about five thousand feet and did a loop. We then did a slow roll. After that I went into a shallow dive and levelled out at about three thousand feet. All I remember is feeling peculiar. The next thing I remember was waking up and I was lying in the hall of Brook Cottage.

The plane had crashed into a spinney at the bottom of my garden. It had landed upside-down. The engine was completely torn away and embedded in the ground. The wings were shattered.

I had blacked out. I knew it could happen when you are doing aerobatics. The blood rushes to the head and this was obviously the cause of my passing out. But it had never happened to me before in an aeroplane. My passenger, helpless in the back seat, was terrified. He thought the plane was skimming the trees rather too close for comfort.

"Aren't we cutting it a bit fine?" he asked nervously over the intercom. I heard nothing.

He looked forward and it seemed to him, according to evidence that he subsequently gave, that I was in a perfectly normal position but when he leaned forward, he could see that my head was slumped forward and I was out cold. We then hit the trees.

Neighbours pulled me out of the demolished Tiger Moth and my passenger emerged, still conscious and unscathed. I had concussion and was taken immediately to hospital. This time it was Audrey's turn to trail after me to the Royal Bucks. But it was really a precaution. I was bruised and had a slight haematoma and that was it. Of course, if the trees had not cushioned the crash, the plane would have gone straight into the ground and it would have been a very different story. We were very lucky.

"David Tomlinson pulled out of this – ALIVE", screamed one newspaper headline framing a photograph of a very dilapidated Tiger Moth, the following day. I hoped that its readers would not share the apparent disappointment! But it was no laughing matter. Officialdom stepped in and I was presented with summonses alleging:

1. I operated an aircraft in a negligent manner so as to endanger life or property.
2. I flew over a congested settlement below fifteen hundred feet.
3. I flew closer than five hundred feet to structures at Mursley.
4. I carried out an aerobatic flight over a populated area.

All of these charges were totally false – but I could understand how they had come about. If I had had a pupil who crashed near his home my reaction would have been simple: I would have had a suspicion that he had been showing off to his family. However, I was not an inexperienced pilot. I was a middle-aged, ex-training instructor who knew better than to take chances. I was not a fool and I was certainly not suicidal. I had flown over the vicinity of the house at a safe height. I had enough experience to know that in a Tiger Moth you can't loop and spin unless you are at a safe height because it always loses height performing aerobatics. A Tiger Moth is not like a Pitts special. That's a high-powered aircraft and if you are clever you can do aerobatics in one of these aircraft quite near the ground. In a Tiger Moth you don't attempt any at less than four to five thousand feet. Still, I could understand the accusations. Even my brother Peter, an experienced Spitfire pilot during the war, should have known me better. He wrote to me and said, "What the hell were you up to?"

The only person who stood by me absolutely staunchly was my ex-commanding officer, Wing Commander O'Donnell, who believed everything I told him. He knew how proud I was of my abilities as a pilot and he also knew that with my experience flying Tiger Moths I wasn't likely to kill myself in one.

The wheels of justice then as now ground slowly. My hearing was not to be until the autumn. Audrey and I went down to Folkestone to stay in a small hotel where I could recuperate from the concussion and watch my bruises heal out of sight.

Jack Minster rang me there. He had a play for me. It was a very commercial, slightly old-fashioned comedy. I invented the title, *Dear Delinquent*.

We opened in Brighton and then came into London to the Westminster Theatre which, being rather off the beaten track, is not noted for being an easy theatre to fill. But *Dear Delinquent* clicked. My father absolutely loved it and used to stand in the foyer as the audience came out. He beamed at complete strangers, "It's very good, isn't it."

We moved to the Aldwych and had a very good run.

Anna Massey in only her second role and perhaps lucky to get it, astonished the management by leaving the play before the end of the run. I never met an actress with more confidence in herself.

By now, my relationship with my father was very different. He was friendly and as I was the only son in England, he relied on me a good deal. I saw a lot of him. He was also delighted with and proud of my success and liked hearing compliments from his friends about me. So everything between us had changed and my miserable childhood was now a dim memory.

CST represented me at the committal proceedings when the local magistrates took depositions from various witnesses. He had no real pretence to advocacy and knew that the inherent weaknesses in the police case were best left uncovered until my trial at Aylesbury Quarter Sessions. Undoubtedly he was right but I found it frustrating to listen to apparently uncontradicted assertions by the Prosecutor and some of the witnesses with which I profoundly disagreed. I was depicted as having done a classic "beat-up".

On Tuesday, October 1st, 1957, I faced the four charges of dangerous flying at Aylesbury, pleading not guilty on all counts. It was a worrying time.

Mr Peter Lewis prosecuting retreated a little from the "beat-up" aspect preferred by his predecessor before the Justices. He said to the jury: "What Mr Tomlinson was doing over Mursley was *possibly* for the benefit of Mrs Tomlinson and the family . . ." Then he added that my general method of flying "was so negligent and careless that there was a likelihood of danger to life and property".

I knew that was untrue but would I be believed?

The hearing lasted two days. Audrey was in court. My father had briefed F. H. Lawton, QC, later to be Lord Justice Lawton. A blue and red toy plane was produced so that witnesses could demonstrate what they had seen. The sight of grown-ups swirling the toy through the air demonstrating as they stood in the witness box what they said I had done would have been comical had it not been so serious. One witness said that she had seen the Tiger Moth over the fields beyond the house. She gyrated the toy plane in an impossible and unlikely demonstration of how she had seen it go higher.

"The engine just seemed to stop and it just twirled down," she said. Down plummeted the toy. More helpfully, it was said that at no time was the plane seen to perform stunts over the village.

Luton Flying Club's chief instructor testified that he was completely satisfied with my competence to fly.

The film of *Three Men in a Boat* had recently opened and in it I had given one of my dim-witted upper-class twit performances as "J". Jimmy Edwards and Laurence Harvey were the other two men in this adaptation of Jerome K. Jerome's classic which turned the polite humour of the original into a successful comedy.

Fred Lawton told the jury, "When you earn your living playing the fool, you like a rest when you get home. That is just the position with Mr Tomlinson. You must not think for one moment that because he earns his living playing the fool for our entertainment that he plays the fool when he is at home. You may think that a man of Mr Tomlinson's age – he is now about forty – married with young children – that the last thing he is going to do is to risk his life and the life of a passenger in the way the prosecution has described. You will hear that if Mr Tomlinson was, in fact, doing what the prosecution witnesses said he was doing he was clearly risking his life – virtually committing suicide. No experienced pilot with Mr Tomlinson's knowledge of flying, especially in Tiger Moths, in which for many years during the war he taught many pupils to fly, would have behaved in the way suggested in this court."

I was cross-examined and told the court exactly what had happened.

"My first manoeuvre was a loop. Then I did a slow roll. I was then over four thousand five hundred feet. I was not over the village at any time. Later I went into a dive and levelled out over two thousand five hundred feet. Then I didn't feel completely well and decided to fly level to recover myself. I was never closer than one thousand yards to the village. I decided to return to Luton and told my passenger. I remember nothing after that."

The Chairman, summing up for the jury, said: "Mr Tomlinson is an experienced flyer and is not likely to have done stunts over his own house to show off."

The jury was out for forty-two minutes and brought back a verdict of not guilty on all counts. My father gave me the thumbs up. The tension of the last six months was gone and I was believed. The jurors, to a man and woman, requested autographs. I felt very peculiar signing autographs in court.

Audrey took the toy plane home from the court for the children and I was at the Westminster Theatre as usual that night, in time for the curtain-up.

Looking back now, I find it hard to understand why the decision was made to charge me, notwithstanding the close proximity between the spot where the plane came down and my home. Long before I was *compos mentis*, my passenger had said that I was clearly unconscious and this was reported the day after the crash. He continued to talk to the press and one remark was reported in a most unfortunate way in the *Daily Telegraph and Morning Post* the day after the verdicts: "I think he will not fly so low again."

I had just been acquitted of deliberately doing that!

The *Daily Mail* got it right. He had said: "I don't think he will ever fly solo again, just in case it should happen a second time."

But he was wrong. One day, later on, I was making a film on location at an aerodrome near Elstree. There was a pilot there with a Tiger Moth.

"Can I do a circuit and landing?" I asked him.

He had never seen me before in his life.

"Certainly," he said.

So off I went. I did a perfect three-point landing and it was just like old times.

I met Peter Sellers in 1957 when we were filming *Up the Creek*. It cost very little to make and was one of the year's successes when it was released.

I played Lt Humphrey Fairweather (according to one critic giving my "normal professional idiot" performance) who, after a series of disastrous attempts to prove to the navy that I have invented a superior rocket, is sent to be commanding officer of HMS *Berkely*, an ancient destroyer mothballed in a remote Suffolk creek. After my first night on board I am awakened by a rooster crowing – on the ship. The crew, captainless for two years, have under the influence of the bosun taken to running rackets with the nearby village. The ship's cook makes pies, the stokehold has been turned into a laundry, a flock of hens produce expensive eggs and pigs are raised for bacon. I, of course, remain blind to all that is going on under my nose.

Peter played the crooked bosun with broken spectacles and an Ulster accent. I was fascinated by him. He was in his early thirties by this time, the only child of a vaudevillian couple. It seems that they had tried to make up for his peripatetic childhood by spoiling him on a massive scale. His mother, Peg, was especially indulgent – nothing was too good for her boy. She was also inordinately possessive, probably because she had lost her first child in infancy. Peter was kept firmly tied to her apron strings. She blackmailed him emotionally and continued to do so even from beyond the grave.

Peter had been a drummer with an ENSA band while still a teenager, he had been a stand-up comic among the nudes at the Windmill Theatre and then he scored a massive success on BBC radio with "The Goons". He was in great demand doing provincial variety but he hated it. It brought back memories of the constant movement and hard cold sheets and the landladies telling him, "Don't touch anything, Sonny."

He was being tipped as a very rare talent. Peter had done television, but his work in films had been only in supporting roles. He was determined to be taken seriously as an actor – a character actor and not just a clown who did funny voices.

His interest in the supernatural and the occult which would eventually take him into spiritualism and mysticism had already begun when we first met. For a time he was content with consulting a clairvoyant who assured him that he would become a big cinema star.

At this time Peter was still married to his first wife, Ann Hayes, an actress who had given up her career to devote herself to Sellers and his. Peter swallowed up a lot of devotion from those close to him. He already had the reputation of being a difficult man, both at home and at work, but as I said, I was absolutely fascinated by him. He was very complex and constantly wary of others taking advantage of him. He took instant offence at imaginary slights. But he was at the same time a very generous man to those who he felt liked him. He took a childish delight in gadgets – cameras and the new-fangled reel-to-reel tape recorders that had just come on the market. He arrived on the set with one.

"Haven't you got one of these?" he asked me as he

demonstrated it.

"No," I said, showing great interest. He was delighted to have someone and something to play with.

As usual in those days I was filming during the day and working in the theatre at night. With my growing family and home I was rather keen on money.

One night, in my dressing-room at the Aldwych (to which *Dear Delinquent* had transferred from the Westminster most successfully, as had my father. He paced the new foyer – "Very good, don't you think? Most enjoyable" he continued to beam at strangers) I found a huge box on my sofa. There was a card on top – "From a friend" was scrawled thereon obviously in a left-handed attempt to disguise the writing. The attempt was most successful. I had no idea who was responsible for the parcel. I opened the box and found an expensive tape recorder. Generous Peter never mentioned that he had sent it but months later he admitted it.

CHAPTER NINE

Uncovering the truth and dreaming of California...

R obert Morley and Robin Fox had formed a production company and they wanted to put on *The Ring of Truth* at the Savoy Theatre. They offered me the lead. The play was about a happily married young woman, played by Margaret Johnson, who superstitiously believes that because she has lost her engagement ring she will lose her happiness. The ring, she feels, was more than a symbol. I was the scientist husband who pooh-poohs the idea. In fact it transpires that the arguments over the loss and her attitude towards it do very nearly destroy the marriage. The critics complained that the comic bits and the philosophical discussions seemed to come from two different plays. Alan Brien called *The Ring of Truth* "a bright, brave, half-successful attempt at an Ibsen comedy". He paid me a nice compliment:

> . . . David Tomlinson as the husband is being and existing . . . we see a glimpse of method acting at its rare best and appreciate for a moment what Mr Browne might have made of his play had it all been acted and written at that level.

The Savoy Theatre was rarely full in the first weeks of the run but then on September 8th Prime Minister Harold Macmillan announced that there would be a general election the following month. He also mentioned that he would be going to the theatre that night to see *The Ring of Truth*. I was lying on my sofa in my dressing-room and I read the news on the front page of the *Evening Standard*. From then on we were full. The Conservatives flourished as well, winning the election on Supermac's slogan "You've never had it so good."

The title of the play turned out to be prophetic. It was during its run that my brother Peter, returning to South Africa from a visit home had his apparition on the way to the airport. Sitting on the top level of a double-decker bus on his way to Heathrow he saw CST sitting up in bed in a strange house in Chiswick drinking a cup of tea.

It was time and long past time, I decided, that we found out exactly what "our father which art in London" was up to. A few years before a friend of mine had tried to follow him, but CST had given him the slip.

At this point CST had taken Audrey to Ascot. In the paddock a small man sidled up to my father and said, "I saw your daughter last week." Audrey noted that CST was somewhat shaken and pretended not to have heard as already she knew of the mystery that surrounded him.

Later at the Junior Carlton Club my father's stockbroker spoke to me. He seemed to want to give me information and mentioned the name of a road where some Tomlinson clients of his lived. It was clear to me that this was the man who had nobbled my father at Ascot. I have never understood why a professional colleague should have wanted to put the boot in for my father in this way.

Soon after, Michael and I were sitting in my flat in London.

"I'm going to look up Tomlinson in the phone book," I said. I picked on the first likely number and rang it. The phone was quickly answered.

"Is that Mrs Tomlinson?" I asked.

"Is that Mr Charles?" I was in turn quizzed.

"No." But I thought that it was an interesting response.

"Oh, you sound just like Mr Charles."

"I wonder if Mrs Tomlinson is in?" I persisted.

"No, she's out shopping – oh, you do sound like Mr Charles."

"Do I? Well, I'll ring back later, thank you very much," I said, and put the phone down. I was obviously on to something. Decidedly excited I could barely wait to ring back. When I did I spoke to a very cagey lady who had obviously been informed about a peculiar man who had rung and sounded just like Mr Charles.

"I do apologise for troubling you," I said. "My name is David Tomlinson. I'm an actor and I'm intrigued to know if we are in any way related."

"Well – um – um . . ."

After a fair amount of stalling she came across. It seemed that my father was her father-in-law. It was difficult to control my astonishment. Although we, in Folkestone, knew nothing of the existence of the London family, they were aware of us. I had struck gold. It was a miracle – and on the first phone call! I invited the lady and her husband to the Savoy the following night. She accepted the invitation. It was difficult to concentrate on the play. What would it be like meeting – my half-brother? I was forty-two years old and had known of his existence for less than twenty-four hours. How much more excited would I have been had I known that I had uncovered the barest tip of the iceberg?

Once the curtain fell I rushed to my dressing-room and awaited my visitors. The lady with whom I had spoken on the phone walked in – with my father's son. He was the image of CST as he appeared in photographs of him as a young subaltern in the First World War. It was a very strange moment for me.

During supper my half-brother mentioned brightly, "Whenever we meet anyone, you can introduce me as your bastard brother!"

I was nonplussed.

"Let's take it in turns," I suggested even more brightly.

Now so many things began to take shape. I now knew why my father had been so keen for me to change my name when he feared there was perhaps a danger that I might become well-known. There would be no way CST could keep the secret from "the other side of the family" as he in later years took to calling his other offspring. There had been interviews with me, and profiles of me published in the newspapers in which my family background had been detailed. Two and two made four and CST could keep the secret from his other children no longer – although it transpired that their mother had never been in the dark. Already the mother of two of his children, she had been devastated by my father's marriage but never deserted him. She stayed with him, bearing five more children. Eventually she changed her name by deed poll and in their narrow circle, always separate from the Folkestone group, they were accepted as man and wife. Later one of her daughters told us she had driven her mother down to look at our home at Folkestone.

Of course, the whole story did not spill out at once, but as we acquired the bones of the story, Michael's genealogical researches filled in the blanks for a time.

During the time CST, as a young man, was articled to the solicitor in Mildenhall, he lodged with a family called Warner. The father of the household, who had been bailiff on a large estate, was a road builder for the council and his wife, as well as running a lodging house, ran a laundry. There were three children, one of whom, Sophie, was two years older than CST. A liaison began then – and it lasted until death, producing seven children. We marvelled at CST's abilities to support two such large families. And we wondered even more that he never got the names mixed up. Logistical difficulties aside, the financial burden had been enormous, for we discovered that neither family suffered financially because of the existence of the other. He was indeed what Robert Morley has called the Great Provider. For us, the Folkestone boys, so many things fell into place with the discovery. CST's inviolate routine – one slip, and confusion would have set in. Now we understood why he insisted that he lived at his club – even after we knew that to be untrue: he had to stick to a single story. It is difficult enough lying, but it is fatal to change one lie for another. We understood now his furtiveness and above all his quick temper. He must have been living on his nerves. The strain of a double life must have been intense.

There was no doubt about it, Sophie knew about us. Later, my father's secretary told me that we often passed on the stairs as she left my father's office and I arrived. But what about my mother? Did she know? It was not the kind of question any of us felt able to ask. Mother had to be protected.

"My mother doesn't know," I told Robert Morley.

"She knows," Robert said.

"But she can't keep a secret. She's not that kind of woman," I insisted.

"This," he said emphatically, "is a secret she has to keep."

"Why?" I asked him, not accepting the possibility.

"Pride," was Robert's succinct reply and he further added that he believed both "wives" knew. Of course he was right; they both knew as later I was able to confirm.

It was some time after the discovery that I was talking to my father and he made his usual reference to living at the club.

"Look," I said to him, "do relax. I know the whole story."

He paled visibly.

"You've nothing to fear from me," I went on. "Your life is your own business. But you don't have to pretend any more."

For once he didn't argue but it was difficult for him not to revert to the old routine.

It seems that Uncle Dick had always known the truth and helped him in his clandestine manoeuvres. However, never once did he betray him – although CST, ever paranoid as only a guilty man can be, suspected that he had. Uncle Dick's wife, sweet Aunt May, had died in 1956. A few years later I went to visit him on what we all thought was his death-bed. He was lying quite still on his back.

"How are you?" I asked.

"Not bad," he said, and after a pause, "I hear you know all about your Daddy."

Rather foolishly Michael had broken the news to him. When Uncle had said, "Your Daddy has a lot on his plate," Michael couldn't resist, "Yes, Uncle, two plates!" Poor Uncle Dick had spent his life covering up for his brother and in the end the truth emerged anyway. CST didn't know how I had found out about the other side of the family, because we all reverted to the pretence, the fantasy he had woven, and at this time never discussed the reality. He blamed Uncle Dick. But he never gave him away as I always later told CST.

Uncle Dick remained silent, gazing up at the ceiling, but after a long time he spoke. "Nothing wrong with your Daddy," he said kindly – and paused. "Nothing." (Longer pause.) "Only one thing wrong with your Daddy – " He paused again, but briefly before adding, "Cunt crazy – but aren't we all?" This seemed to me hilariously funny and so unexpected.

The next thing we knew Uncle Dick rose up, went out and bought a new bed – a double one – and he married his nurse.

We were astounded.

"Married? Uncle Dick married? But he can't walk," exclaimed young David.

"She's not at all like your Auntie May," Uncle Dick said as we chatted in his sitting-room one day. "She's a bit of a cow, old boy and I have to keep an eye on her." Edith sat there throughout the conversation while he listed her faults. Women seemed to put up with a lot from CST and his brother.

I was in my dressing-room at the Savoy one night and I got a message saying that Walt Disney was coming to see the play and that if I was free would I have dinner with him afterwards.

I immediately suspected a Morley leg pull. He was a master of the phoney message. I had fallen completely for the threatened legal action he had invented which purportedly had come from my South African friends that terrifying night when we were in *The Little Hut,* and there were further incidents to fuel my suspicions. On one occasion when I was making a film at Elstree I had a slight altercation with the director Henry Cass (whom many referred to as the Cass of death). I arrived at the Lyric for the evening's performance still irritated over the encounter and told Robert about it. The following day when I arrived at the studio there was a telegram from Cass on my dressing-table apologising profusely for his behaviour and admitting that the fault was totally his. I was mollified. When I arrived on the set Cass greeted me, holding a telegram. "It was awfully good of you but quite unnecessary. I completely understand."

What on earth was he talking about?

"Your telegram," he said. "So generous of you and of course I accept your apology wholeheartedly, though," he added again, "it is totally unnecessary."

I was holding his telegram to me. It didn't take me long to work out just who had been responsible for the two identical communications. In fact he was sitting up in bed at my flat eating Alice's breakfast at that moment, gleefully chuckling at the thought of the two telegrams coming together. I never discussed my days at the studio with Robert from that day onwards.

I checked with the company director. "Is Walt Disney by any chance out front tonight?" I asked cautiously.

"He certainly is," came the reassurance.

Images of Hollywood contracts danced before my eyes.

Disney came round after the show. He was very formal.

"I enjoyed the play very much, Mr Tomlinson," he said. "I hope you are free to join us for dinner."

"Yes, please," I said.

There were six of us. One, an elderly gentleman in a dinner jacket, sported an incongruous Texan-style string tie with his formal wear. I never discovered his identity. About halfway through dinner all of a sudden apropos of absolutely nothing he began, "I want to say this, Walt, I want to say this right here and now. Walt. You are a genius. I want to say it and no one is going to stop me."

No one made the slightest attempt to stop him.

"You, Walt," he went on, "are a genius . . ." and he continued in this vein. I suppose Walt was a man who could take flattery as well as any of us, but I thought this fellow was overdoing it and was never going to stop. When he finally did, after a pause I found myself saying, "You did very well, but don't do it again."

Everyone laughed and of course I felt immediately sorry for the old fellow in the string tie. I don't know what possessed me to interrupt his lavish praises, except that to my English ears someone had to say something.

Soon everyone was dancing and I was left alone at the table with Disney.

"Where are you going now?" he asked me.

"Home," I said. Unless of course he wants me on the first plane to Los Angeles, I thought.

"Where's home?"

"In the country." Most nights after the show I drove back to Mursley. The forty-five-mile drive to Buckinghamshire was soothing at that time of night when the traffic had gone, and Audrey would leave me supper on a tray and then, if I wasn't filming, I could sleep late in the morning. I envisaged arriving home that night and waking her up to tell her the exciting news. We were going to California.

"Come and have a drink," Walt said and my hopes remained high. Of course he wouldn't want to discuss business in such a public place. We walked up the road to the Dorchester Hotel where he was staying in the Oliver Messel suite. I was immediately taken by the fact that the suite was untouched. It was as if no one was staying there. Disney was a man without side. He travelled with a toothbrush and a pair of pyjamas.

I later learned that the film he was about to shoot

concerned an English family in Paris. It was called *Bon Voyage*. Walt poured himself a large whiskey and because of the drive ahead I declined to join him, but we chatted most amiably about the play, about films and about families. The next thing I knew we had said good night and I was in the lift going down to the lobby. Fred McMurray eventually got the part. Should I, I wondered, have refrained from interrupting the old fellow in the string tie?

On my birthday, May 7th, 1960 Audrey presented me with our third son – an especially beautiful, especially perfect little boy. David and Jamie were delighted to have another brother. None of us had the slightest inkling as we cuddled William what an enormous effect he would have on all of us.

CHAPTER TEN

In which I fall in love with Hollywood...

I thought *Boeing-Boeing* was the worst play I had ever read. I wanted nothing to do with it even though I was at a loose end but the producer John Gale was flattering in his persistence that I should change my mind.

He consulted me about directors of comedy and I recommended Jack Minster. Within hours Jack had read it and was on the phone.

"Don't you want to be in a success? Are you mad? This one will make a fortune."

I was somewhat taken aback, as I had bargained on Jack hating it. So keen was he that he invited me to dinner that very night. I was duly impressed and somewhat surprised, as he had never done so before.

"Have dinner with me at the RAC and let's talk," said Jack.

I agreed to meet him. I was so sure I could arrange it so that he would realise that I was wrong for the part. Nobody in my life had ever impressed me more than Jack Minster. He was a brilliant director of comedy and we seemed to spark each other off and were very successful together. Those who didn't know him were mistaken in thinking him a gloomy character. How wrong they were. Nobody ever made me laugh more than Jack.

When we walked into the restaurant the head waiter told me that my father was there. Jack was not then keen for any distraction from this important meeting and so it proved to be.

"I must say hello to my Dad," I insisted and as I approached his table I saw that he was not alone. With him sat a woman who looked like my mother. She dressed like my mother but she was not my mother. I realised immediately it was "the other woman". I also understood in that split second of recognition that he controlled her as he controlled my mother. She was dressed darkly. My father insisted that everyone over whom he had any influence had to be dressed in navy-blue or black. He himself never wore anything but dark grey, black or navy-blue and always wore absolutely plain stiff formal collars – not merely for the office, always.

My father paled visibly on my approach. Tentatively he half rose and greeted me as effusively as he could manage in his confused state. Turning to his guest he paused. "This," he said indicating the woman, "this . . ." He paused once more. "This is . . . Mrs Gibson."

I knew very well who it was. But for CST to have plucked that particular name from the air was most amusing. There was a fairly well-known music-hall comedian of the thirties called Claud Dampier who always introduced a lady of dubious origin by the name Mrs Gibson. CST's subconscious must have gone into overdrive at my unexpected appearance. After a little small talk I joined Jack at a very unadjacent table and proceeded to tell him the story of CST. He was duly fascinated. Jack was particularly interested that one of CST's first houses in which he lived with "the lady" was in Kew.

"Yes, Kew. So respectable," he muttered thoughtfully. "It's not such an unusual story," he added. "There's always been a lot of it about."

Somehow by the end of the evening because of my respect for Jack I had agreed to do *Boeing-Boeing*. I was still convinced that it had no chance of coming into London. The tour was very successful as it turned out, but as I had predicted we folded on the road. A London theatre could not be found for the production. In fact, all the London theatres positively fought not to have us. I was relieved. I had grown to like the play a little better but I knew the audiences loved it. Then John Gale rang me full of excitement. "We've got the Apollo – and we've got to open in a fortnight."

"Not with me," I said. "It's not possible." The play had to be re-cast.

Later I agreed reluctantly, provided they had the entire set, furniture and props set up at the Metropolitan Theatre (now demolished) on the Edgware Road where John had arranged the fortnight's rehearsal. I never thought they'd manage it but they did.

We opened at the Apollo Theatre on February 20th, 1962. Half an hour before the curtain went up two of the handles fell off the door. The whole play depended on the doors opening and closing. There was chaos backstage but somehow the handles got fixed back on.

Boeing-Boeing got some very commercial notices. Bernard Levin said, "I think I'll go by boat" but strangely he said it in a way that brought audiences into the theatre. And T. C. Worsley reported:

> But the extra little touch which will probably mean success comes from David Tomlinson as the naive provincial friend who learns the facts of life very quickly . . . there is nothing routine about Mr Tomlinson's comedy. It has that touch of artistry which comes from imagination and inventiveness.

So much for my theatrical prescience. *Boeing-Boeing* eventually ran for two thousand and thirty-five performances. It was my fifth theatrical success in a row. If I had known it was to be my last I would have tried to enjoy it more.

During *Boeing-Boeing*, Tony Richardson came backstage to enlist me for the part of Lord Fellamar in the film of "Tom Jones".

In one scene, I had to attempt to rape Susannah York. Tony was not always on the set by this time. He was it seems concentrating on a play for Olivier called *Semi Detached* which proved for both of them to be a rare disaster.

Whenever I found him, I asked him what he wanted of me.

"Do anything you like!" was his instruction which seemed to me to be rather rash.

"Put your hand up her skirt!" he shouted during the rape scene. Poor Susannah was not pleased and somewhat anxious but I was able to reassure her by word and deed.

Hugh Griffiths, who was well remembered for his Squire Western in the film, used to arrive with a carload of dogs having been up all night. His powers of recuperation, however, were excellent. Walking beside Edith Evans while shooting a scene with her on location in Holland Park, he said – she thought quite seriously – "I am going to pitch you into that pond!" She was understandably rather nervous of him.

Our fourth son Henry was born on July 3rd, 1962. Louise, Sister Noakes, arrived as usual to minister to mother and child. She had great experience with sick children and she was especially interested in them. Willie was just over two when Henry was born and during her time with us, Louise suggested very gently that perhaps Willie was not progressing as he should. It was true that he seemed different from David and Jamie but then we reasoned that all children develop at their own pace. Actually Willie had walked quicker than the other two. He had never actually crawled – just got onto his feet and walked. But it was no good making comparisons. Louise again suggested that Willie might be deaf but Audrey was sure this was not the case. When he was in his pram in the garden, the place he seemed to like best, where he could watch the trees and wave at the shadows, Audrey would tap on the window-pane and he would turn and look at her. There was nothing wrong with his hearing, we decided, he was just a slow developer. Lots of children didn't talk by the age of two. But as the months passed we were less and less convinced that all was as it should be. He became aggressive – hitting out in frustration at his inability to make us understand what he wanted. He pulled baby Henry's hair until we thought the poor child would have none left. He would also stand with his back to a door and kick away at it with his heels.

Audrey took him to a Harley Street specialist who declared that he was deaf. Unconvinced, she went to Guy's Hospital where the diagnosis of deafness was perfunctorily confirmed. But Audrey could not accept this. Her own observation was that Willie responded to sound – and she saw him all the time, not for a few minutes in the unnatural surroundings of a doctor's surgery or a hospital.

While Audrey was making this first, rather desperate round of professional people, I was five thousand miles away in Hollywood. The summons had come from Disney – belated surely, but it had come.

I had been lying in bed one morning and Audrey brought me a cup of coffee. "They want you to go to Hollywood!" was her wake-up greeting.

Hollywood offers in the past had not been taken seriously and anyway I had never been free when they occurred as I was under contract to the Rank Organisation. As I had been to the *Evening Standard* Drama Awards the night before and had drunk rather a lot, which was unlike me, and I was feeling rather muzzy, I asked Audrey what on earth she was talking about.

"They want you to go to Hollywood," she repeated. "Maud Spector is expecting you in her office this morning to talk about it. I told her to treat you with care, that you'd had a bad night."

Maud Spector ran Disney's London casting office.

I stirred myself and made my way to the office. Luckily we were in London so it was only two hundred yards to walk. I walked in and barely had time to sit down when Maud began, "Let's get right down to business. We can do the social stuff later. They want you to go to Hollywood. Can you get out of *Boeing-Boeing*?"

"Yes, I can leave whenever I want."

"Good. Here's the script. They'll fly you and the family out to the coast. They'll give you a house and pay all expenses and they'll pay you . . ."

She named a heart-warming sum.

"Of course," she continued in the same breath, "you don't have to make up your mind right away."

I was dazed. "Tell me again," I said.

She did so.

I couldn't believe it. I clutched the script of *Mary Poppins* to my bosom and hurried home to Audrey.

Boeing-Boeing continued its phenomenal run. I prepared for my flight to Disney. It might have been two years since I had anticipated the summons from Walt, but better late than never. Audrey would come out later with the children.

"The first thing they'll do is take you to a piano," Audrey warned, "and make sure you can sing."

Besides making extremely successful films and constructing marvellous parks, the Disney organisation is wonderful at cosseting its employees. I flew first of all to New York where they had kindly arranged for me to see *Tovarich* on Broadway. It starred Vivien Leigh and I liked her performance. The organisation was perfect and the following morning I was flown on to Los Angeles. In no time at all I was at the studio where I met Bill Walsh, the film's producer. He had arrived in Hollywood a considerable time before I did – 1934 to be precise. At first he had written radio shows and newspaper columns. He'd also been an advertising writer and a PR man before he joined Disney where he co-produced the Mickey Mouse Club and the television series, *Davy Crockett*.

"Now what have we got here?" I could see him thinking as we were introduced. He had a very good look and almost immediately called in Irwin Kostel, the musical director. Irwin carried a score under his arm.

As Audrey had predicted I found myself standing by a piano. I sang a couple of bars.

"That's fine," Irwin said, "let's go and see what's happening on the set."

Is that it, I thought. "Don't you want to hear some more?" I asked.

"No."

"You didn't give me much of a chance."

"It's fine. You can sing," he said laconically.

They certainly make up their minds quickly, I thought. A very professional lot, these Disneyites.

Strangely enough, Glynis Johns was playing my wife in *Mary Poppins*. We seemed to be fated to meet up professionally every ten or fifteen years. I began to feel we had grown up together – in *Quiet Wedding*, would-be lovers in *Miranda* and now man and wife for Disney. I seemed also to be surrounded by child stars. Both Glynis and Julie Andrews had first trod the boards aged twelve. They had grown up, but at times I thought the two children who played my son and daughter were as mature as any of us. That, of course, could be expected from Karen Dotrice who came from an acting family.

Matthew Garber, however, was another matter. His father was in the rag trade and slightly mystified by the whole business. Matt was simply a natural, and highly intelligent. It didn't take him long to realise the power he wielded in this expensive production.

"My Dad's coming to lunch," he said to me one day, "would you like to come with us?"

"Are you paying?" I asked.

He thought about it for a minute. "OK," he decided, very seriously.

As we went in, the lady in charge of the executive restaurant said, "How do you do, Sir." She wasn't addressing me, but Matt.

His charming father was quite surprised. "Why does that woman call you Sir?" he asked his son.

"Because," Matt said, drawing himself up to his full three and a half feet, "I'm playing a very important part in this picture." Later I told his father that Matt was simply stating the absolute truth.

Just occasionally the power went to his head . . . and he picked his moment carefully. He didn't balk at a small scene but waited until a large crowd had been assembled on the set. Dozens waited while Matt suddenly said, "I don't feel like doing it today."

Panic ensued. I managed to persuade him that with power came responsibility.

It was three months before Audrey and the children arrived. During that time I saw a lot of Irwin Kostel who also awaited his wife's arrival. He was a lovely man and a brilliant musician. He had been musical director of *Fiorello* and *A Funny Thing Happened To Me On The Way To The Forum* on Broadway. He already had an Academy Award for the film of *West Side Story*. (He went on to win a second Oscar for *The Sound of Music*.)

Irwin and I led a happy bachelor existence. He introduced me to the pleasures of shopping and eating in Los Angeles. We explored the delightful Farmer's Market and I loved every minute of it. Often Julie Andrews, a new mother, took me under her wing as well. She cooked for me while I occasionally held the baby.

Audrey arrived with the children – David was nine, Jamie seven, William three and Henry still in arms with Valmai Thomas, their nanny. We moved into a lovely house, courtesy of Walt, overlooking the San Fernando Valley and we couldn't have liked it more. As we had four children Walt insisted on a pool with an electric cover. When closed the children could run across it. It was not all that usual at the time. I found America wonderfully stimulating and Audrey agreed with me – she has often said that the best holidays are arranged by film companies. And it was true this time – nothing was too much trouble for Walt and Co.

I had told Bill Walsh the news about Willie.

"They insist he's deaf," I said, "but Audrey and I just

don't think he is."

Bill told Disney who I then learned had, with Spencer Tracy, founded the John Tracy Clinic for the Deaf. John was Tracy's son, who had been born deaf and now worked at the Disney studio.

Walt came to me one day.

"If you like," he said, "when your son arrives I can arrange for him to be seen." This he kindly did.

We arrived at the clinic and Willie was taken into a cubicle with a charming young girl. We spent the morning there while she put him through a series of tests.

"I don't like to criticise anyone," she finally said referring to our English consultants, "and I don't know why you were told he is deaf, but your son is certainly not deaf."

Audrey and I exchanged a glance. We were grateful. The doctors were wrong and we were right.

"But," she continued, "he probably does have a problem."

So deafness had been ruled out – but what was wrong? Audrey and I found ourselves on the interminable road that people with handicapped children have to walk.

Walt Disney was a fascinating man. He was a shrewd business man and a creative innovator but his success stemmed from the fact that he never exchanged his Midwestern simplicity for West Coast sophistication. Walt was born in Chicago and after a spell with the Red Cross during the First World War, settled for a time in Kansas City earning his living as a commercial artist. He was obviously an immensely successful and wealthy man when I knew him but his work was still his pleasure and he had few others except for one large whiskey at the end of the day. He drove a Thunderbird and he had no need in the studio of Renoirs on the wall or Rolls-Royces. He insisted that everyone call him Walt, which actually made some employees rather uneasy. Everyone knew that Disney was an autocratic man capable, if necessary, of being ruthless when it came to the job. If someone had to go, they went – no matter what personal involvements were at stake. The job came first and if Walt felt someone wasn't performing, wasn't pulling his weight, even if that person had been at the studio for years, he unleashed his hatchetmen. Disney always had the last word – except, it seemed, at home.

On his first arrival in Hollywood in 1923, he had tried unsuccessfully to produce a cartoon series of *Alice* pictures combining cartoon characters with live actors. One of the actresses in this series was Lillian Bounds who soon became Mrs Disney. It was she who later helped him create the character of Mickey Mouse – the rodent on which the empire had been built.

Walt had a miniature steam railway installed in his garden and he loved nothing more than putting on his engineer's cap and put-putting around the grounds.

"Mrs Disney doesn't like the train," he told me rather sadly one day. "She thinks it is bad for the roses."

The next thing I heard was that the train had gone.

It seems there were a number of Walt's passions which were not shared by Mrs Disney. When he had been struggling to complete the first feature-length cartoon film, *Snow White and the Seven Dwarfs*, he ran out of money. All the Hollywood moguls were delighted at his discomfiture, willing the upstart to fail.

Walt showed his wife the half-finished film.

She startled him. "I don't like dwarfs anyway," she told him.

Luckily for Walt, indeed for the movie-going public, Mrs Disney was wrong. The money was raised and Disney was launched as a major force in the entertainment industry. He had a faith in himself and an unswerving vision, as well as courage and tenacity. When he said he was going to build Disneyland, he was told he was mad. When he announced he was going to build another sound stage his accountants told him he couldn't afford it. But Walt always prevailed. He knew how to run a studio. He never lost sight of his masterplan and tempered that with an acute attention to detail. He had been known to walk into the publicity department, stoop and pick up a paper-clip from the floor.

"Those cost money, you know," he said simply, depositing it on the nearest desk.

He was always two steps ahead of everyone in the, by this time, vast organisation, although he seldom rubbed it in.

Bill Walsh told me that it was he who "discovered" me for Disney. "He had never seen you," Bill said. "Until I showed him *Up the Creek* and then he agreed we should get you for the part."

Walt had never told him about *The Ring of Truth* nor our meeting two years before. Bill was flabbergasted, but it was typical of Walt to be one jump ahead.

Disney invited Audrey and the two older children to lunch at the studio one day. We were ushered into his office which was a treasure trove.

Audrey thanked him for the wonderful time they had been having. Walt had laid on trips all over the place. We had been to his ranch and had the VIP treatment at Disneyland.

"Have you been to Palm Springs?" Walt asked.

"No," said Audrey.

"Oh, you must go to Palm Springs. You'll love it. Dolores – " he summoned his secretary. "You can fly up in my plane." Audrey protested but it was useless. He was determined and he told Dolores to organise it right away. Walt never procrastinated.

Seven-year-old Jamie noticed a model plane on Disney's desk.

"Is that your plane?" he asked.

"Why, yes it is," Walt said, pleased by the question. It was indeed a perfect model.

Jamie paused a moment. He was thinking. Then his face lit up. "Do you magic it to make it bigger?" he asked.

Disney was entranced by Jamie's question. Nothing in the world could have pleased him more.

"Yeh," he said slowly, playing with the idea, "yeh, that's

what I do. I magic it big."

"Magic it now," Jamie demanded.

Walt thought for a moment. "Not here, Jamie, the room is too small."

We were soon jetting in Disney's plane to Palm Springs with Chuck the pilot in constant touch on the intercom with Jamie.

When we arrived back in Hollywood Jamie warned his new friend, "Chuck, when Walt magics the plane back into his office you be sure you're not in it."

This of course was reported to Disney. He came down to see me on the set. He seldom visited the set and when he did it was always very casual usually wandering around throwing peanuts or popcorn into his mouth, although in his quiet way he took in everything that was happening.

"Dear Jamie. A reaction like that means more to me than I can say," he told me. Delighting children of all ages was Walt's business and it thrilled him to see it work at close hand.

Having finished my role as Mr Banks, Bill had me doing voices for the picture. I'm the voice of the bosun in it and also the parrot at the end.

With Walt, Bill and Audrey I saw a rough cut of *Mary Poppins* before returning to England. I thought it was appallingly sentimental and that it must be a failure and very nearly said, "Well, Walt, you can't win them all."

But I was wrong about that film as Mrs Disney had been about *Snow White*. Walt very nearly did win them all. He didn't like admitting it but of course he was blessed with the common touch. What he liked was what the public liked and obviously that's one of the many reasons why he was so successful.

A charming and fascinating memory I have of Walt Disney is being given a personal demonstration by him of the mechanics and workings of one of the three unclothed prototypes of Abraham Lincoln. Lincoln would stand up from a sitting position, cough politely with a hand over his mouth and speak the Gettysburg Address.

Always interested and very knowledgeable about machines, the great man knew exactly how it worked and he was like a child with a toy train: touchingly pleased to show me everything, but frequently apologising and assuring me that the finished product would be just fine. The Lincoln figure was one of the many mechanical wonders designed and built at Disney's engineering works (known as WED) for the World Fair and later to be permanent fixtures at Disneyland.

Shortly after this I received a letter dated February 23rd, 1965 from Gene Fowler Jnr, President of the American Cinema Editors' 15th Annual Dinner. I was invited to attend, but was unable to accept due to work in England. The happy outcome was that my English friend, Peter Ellenshaw, the brilliant special-effects designer and Oscar winner, long settled in California and married to an American ex-nurse, the delightful Bobbie, received the "Eddy" on my behalf. This was an award given to me by the American Cinema Editors for the best début in a US film. The other nominees were Stanley Holloway in *My Fair Lady*, Harve Presnell in *The Unsinkable Molly Brown*, John Leyton in *Guns of Batasi*, and Donnelly Rhodes in *Ten Minutes from Now*.

I was delighted to win the award but lucky, I feel, to be preferred to Stanley Holloway. It is considerably larger than an Oscar and has ever since taken pride of place in my office. When asked, "Is that an Oscar?", I always say, "No, better!"

Thanks to Walt we returned to England armed with the knowledge that our third son wasn't deaf – but with no real idea what was wrong with him – although as time went on it became more and more apparent that there was something very wrong. We were faced with an enormous problem.

CHAPTER ELEVEN

*Learning
and coping –
with death
and disability...*

Willie was growing stronger and bigger and still not speaking and soon we didn't have an undamaged door in the house. With a rhythmic kicking of his heels he bashed them all in. We did a round of professionals and found little help. One consultant, after examining Willie, said the best thing we could do was put him away in a home and forget about him.

"He's a write-off," we were told perfunctorily. It is difficult to believe it now but that is what he said. We couldn't accept that diagnosis. Surely there was some way of getting through to him. There had to be. But we had no idea how to begin. Still we retained our hope in spite of pessimistic doctors.

We weren't getting much help on the home front either. My parents said it was just a case of not knowing how to handle him. Typically, CST said, "Lacking in discipline, that's the trouble." But he soon realised he was wrong. My mother was gentler in approach but equally thwarted by Willie's introversion.

Then, by some miracle, when Willie was about seven years old we met an extraordinary lady, a Montessori teacher, Sybil Elgar. In desperation we visited her. We clutched at many, many straws. Willie had virtually no speech and his frustration grew daily. Poor Henry, number four, to our shame took a back seat at this time as all our attentions were concentrated on Willie and his problems. It is some credit to Henry that he has flourished in spite of what must have been some neglect. Also our calm, cheerful nanny, Valmai, was wonderful with all the boys. David and Jamie, now at prep school in the next village, were getting on with their lives as schoolboys will. Between our inability to communicate with Willie (Audrey always had a marvellous instinctive bond with the children), his anti-social behaviour and her feelings of guilt, she was having difficulty sleeping and was distraught. Having been told he was a write-off, which despite the evidence of our eyes, we refused to accept, there was still no clue as to what was wrong with him and if we couldn't discover what was wrong how could we even begin to fix it? Then we learned the word – autism.

Even now, autism remains very much a mystery to the medical profession, so perhaps I shouldn't be too harsh on those consultants who were so totally wrong when we saw them nearly thirty years ago. However, the lack of sympathy, the total inhuman response we encountered, still rankles. The condition is more readily diagnosed now but still there is no consensus about the way to deal with it. The name of the disorder itself led to confusion, especially among the general public. It is taken from the Greek "auto" meaning self, and was first used by an American psychologist only in 1944 when he noted a striking characteristic common to children similarly afflicted. They had, he decided, the look of a person lost in daydreams. Autistics avoid eye contact with others and seem pensive and totally absorbed in their own thoughts.

Autism is, fortunately, a very rare condition. It can manifest itself in many ways but there are some common factors. It occurs mainly in boys and becomes apparent by the time the child is two and a half, at the oldest. He evinces social withdrawal and speaks very little, if at all.

By the late nineteen seventies researchers had concluded that autism was most likely the result of abnormalities in the central nervous system coupled with a metabolic defect. In other words it is a physical handicap resulting in lack of development of certain mental abilities. In the early nine-teen sixties, where we were, the powers that pontificate insisted on a monumental absurdity, namely that it was due to faulty upbringing – it was due to cold, unresponsive parents. We didn't need that. Audrey felt more guilty but I was unconvinced and pointed to the other three perfectly normal sons. There was nothing withdrawn about them. Then, most experts thought that autistic children were in-capable of being educated. Now they have changed their minds. Now the experts say that sympathetic but formal and structured schooling brings results. They certainly do – I can vouch for that – and luckily for us, and especially for Willie, Mrs Elgar knew that instinctively.

Sybil Elgar had started, of her own volition, a smallish unit for autistic children in a house in Ealing, London. She had real talent for getting through the barriers. Autistic children live like an egg in a shell, and Mrs Elgar could pierce that shell. No one could totally crack it – that is the nature of the affliction – but with infinite patience she managed to break through. She taught Willie to use a pencil, to listen to music. He gradually developed a few words. He spent some days each week at Ealing but frequently came home – both we and Sybil made sure of that. Gradually he became a member of the family instead of the complete focus of worried attention. It all took a lot of time but he learned to share and we gave thanks for Mrs Elgar who we deemed not only a genius but a saint. Of course, nothing happens overnight, especially with autism, and usually Henry, as the youngest, had to bear the worst of Willie's outbursts. He used to look forward to Willie coming home from his school and then when he did return as often as not Willie would grab Henry by the hair. All crayons and drawing materials had to be hidden away when Willie was in residence as in the early days he practised his newly acquired skill with dogged persistence (obsessional, repetitious behaviour is another characteristic of autism), covering any available surface with drawings – walls, doors, furniture, carpets – everything. But at least we were making some progress. There was hope. We couldn't have imagined at that time how far Willie would progress. We simply were grateful for the proof that he wasn't a write-off.

My first job back in England was in a film called *The Truth about Spring*. I played the millionaire uncle of the young man who was part of the love interest. It was a truly dreadful film but with my new-found Hollywood cachet I was billed as making a "Guest Appearance" in nice big block capitals.

Soon after, I was back in the West End – albeit briefly – at the Globe Theatre in *Mother's Boy*, a rather complicated play written by a good friend, Sewell Stokes. Sewell had written, with his brother Leslie, *Oscar Wilde*, the play in which Robert Morley had scored his first triumphant success thirty years previously. I also directed the play, which some critics thought was unwise, but I don't think that was the reason for its failure. As the critic John Percival pointed out, "Now every schoolboy knows, of course, the ramifications and intricacies of the relationships between Nero, Poppaea and Agrippina, but unfortunately theatre audiences are not made up of schoolboys."

That year my father's structured life began to collapse as well. I learned about this much later. At the time my father hid his very real sorrow as successfully as he had hidden the truth about his life from us all those years. He had developed deception to a fine art.

CST was at his London home with Sophie when she had a massive stroke. He managed to get her into bed and called the doctor who arrived none too quickly. After examining the 85-year-old woman, the doctor said there was nothing that could be done for her. She lingered for a while, virtually unaware of her surroundings, but, CST was assured, in no pain. Just before her death, she managed to recognise the man to whom she had given her life – the man she had had to share for all those years. He was pleased that she recognised him.

Sophie's death put an end to the need for subterfuge. CST could of course have returned to Folkestone on a permanent basis. He was after all retired, but so used was he to his double life that he kept to his routine, often spending his days in London at his club playing bridge.

Sophie had remained extremely healthy until suffering the fatal stroke but Mother, in Folkestone, was more or less bedridden although she was seven years younger than the other woman.

One day Audrey and I were visiting her there. She was sitting up in bed going through a small old-fashioned leather case which was full of family bits and pieces. Suddenly she produced an aged bit of paper. It had obviously been much handled over the years.

"What do you think of that?" she asked, handing it to me.

It dated from the First World War and had been written by my father from France. It had been written to Sophie but posted to my mother. The chatty missive left no doubt about the relationship they shared.

CST came into the room.

"I've just been showing David *that* letter," she said, acting her Marie Lohr role.

"What letter, darling?" he asked innocently.

"*That* letter."

She handed it to him and he read it without haste, slowly turning it over as it was a long letter filling both sides. After a pause, without comment, he put it down and left the room. My mother's letter had gone to Sophie. CST confirmed this much later. It was interesting to discover that she was pregnant with me at the time.

I watched my mother very closely and her steely expression said everything. The years of resentment were plain to see. I remember this so well, and nothing before or since made more of an impression on me.

That my father had managed to put the wrong letter into the envelope addressed to my mother did not surprise me. He was always an untidy man despite his fastidiousness in dress. But had she never before told him of it? Had she kept the knowledge to herself for sixty years, only letting him know she knew on her death-bed? Had her love and loyalty been so intense, or was it – as Robert Morley had said – her pride that forced her to carry the secret? This was probably such that she would have found it impossible to carry on the marriage had she told him that she knew of his deception. The marriage was important to her. So, I suppose, was this supreme act of one-upmanship on her death-bed.

Although she had become slowly bedridden, my mother's later life had been much enlivened by visits to Michael and his family in Ceylon, to Peter in Cape Town and to relatives in Orkney.

When my mother died, CST seemed relieved, but he had been very attentive, as was always the case when she was ill. He was now eighty-six years old and had spent more than fifty-five of those years bringing up two families at the same time, always trying to keep two women, if not happy, then at least content. As he told me later, he had done his best. Now he could relax. In his latter years he mellowed enormously. The pressure was finally off him. He spent most of his time in Folkestone. Mrs Matty continued as housekeeper. She had looked after both my parents for nearly forty years and she was devoted to them equally. Mrs Matty was advanced in age herself and practically stone deaf.

One thing Father refused to give up was driving. He had always been an appalling driver and, not surprisingly, his skills did not improve with age. He managed to write off three cars. I was always trying to get him to stop, but it was no use confronting CST head-on about anything. It just made him more determined to get his own way. So I tried subtlety.

"You know," I said to him one day, "when I'm driving I find my reactions are not as good as they used to be."

"Mine are better," he countered and that was the end of that conversation.

I tried another tactic.

"Why don't you get a driver?" I asked, adding quickly, "You can afford it and you could get a lady driver."

CST never lost his interest for the opposite sex, and indeed even in his advanced years women still seemed to find him attractive. I once asked his secretary, Miss Young, if there had been others besides the two who shared his life.

"Only casuals," she replied.

My idea of a lady driver intrigued him. He paused and thought about it. "I might rather like that," he admitted. But he continued to drive himself erratically around the south coast, and to his house in London and back to Folkestone.

One day he rang me up.

"I thought you'd be pleased to know I'm giving up driving," he said.

I was delighted and silently thanked heaven. CST was certainly a menace on the roads. But what had finally convinced him?

"Well, I had a little bit of an accident," he said. "My car was in collision with a builder's lorry." He usually used solicitor speak. "But," he hastily assured me, "I'm all right."

"How's the builder?" I asked.

"He's all right."

"How's the car?"

CST paused. "I suppose you would call it a write-off."

This was the second Jaguar he had written off, but it was a relief to know that at last he was off the roads.

Father changed his mind. Six weeks later he bought a Mercedes. We were dumbfounded.

Eventually his doctor, for whom he had little use except to supply him with sleeping pills and certify him capable of driving, refused the certificate. That didn't stop CST: although he was ninety-three and unlicensed, he continued to drive – usually on the wrong side of the road. Eventually the police caught up with him on the Maidstone by-pass. He was summonsed and I rang up a solicitor he knew, who agreed to represent him – gratis. The solicitor drove him to Maidstone, represented him in court and managed to get him off with a fifty-pound fine.

CST's only comment was, "I could have handled it much better myself." I was truly amazed. He was not at all grateful for the trouble his colleague had taken, but then gratitude was seldom a part of his nature. I, however, was very grateful that at long last he was really finally off the road.

CST took to travelling after both his ladies had died and often went to visit Peter in South Africa. Like me, Peter discovered that CST, who had so terrified us all in our youth, now, with his cares lifted, became very good company. He had a good sense of humour and even into his nineties continued to be very popular with women. It seemed he could charm and amuse them. This he always managed too with my mother whose adoration and loyalty continued until her death despite everything.

CST, however, never learned to respond to the finer things of life. I quote my brother Michael:

> CST was bigoted to an extreme. His own views on any subject were the right ones and final. There was no point in debating any issue with him. He was a materialist and a cynic and never failed to look behind and to see through any form of pretension. His interest in such things as art, music or religion was negligible. We, his children, derived absolutely nothing from him so far as these things were concerned. Here the word philistine must inevitably come to mind. Such outside interests as he had were limited to horse racing and certain historical figures, particularly Napoleon and Hitler, about whom he read avidly but spasmodically.

One thing he never gave up was his search for the perfect piece of beef. This was the only perfection he ever sought. When Peter showed him Table Mountain, CST hardly bothered to look at the well-known wonder before him. "Lovely, old boy, what's for lunch?"

Peter, too, was fascinated by CST's life. Who could fail to be? Now that both women were dead, he felt it could be discussed. And CST talked to him easily. Peter, I repeat, had always been his favourite.

"You know," he told Peter, "I don't consider myself an immoral man. I loved two women, that's all."

"But what about all those children?" Peter asked.

"Ah, well," he sighed, "when you're in love . . ."

"But you married the wrong woman," Peter persisted.

"No," CST said, "as soon as I set eyes on your mother I wanted to marry her. She was beautiful and irresistible."

I continued my West End losing streak playing Sir John Holt in William Douglas Home's *A Friend Indeed* at the Cambridge and as Dr Jack Kingsley in *The Impossible Years* at the same theatre seven months later. The former I liked enormously. At his best William Douglas Home is a magical playwright – witness the delicate gossamer of *The Kingfisher*. At his worst, he is still good. One could not say the same of *The Impossible Years*. That was truly dreadful. It was written by Bob Fisher and Arthur Marx, son of Groucho. The producer, Emile Littler, sent me to New York to see it, where it was running on Broadway. Sam Levine was playing the lead. I thought it was terrible, but in fairness that had been my reaction to *Boeing-Boeing*. Anyway, Littler persuaded me with money. He had faith in the play even if I didn't and offered me a non-returnable advance to play the part. No matter what happened, I would get paid. It was an offer I couldn't refuse. Littler took the gamble – and lost. It was a disaster. I played a psychiatrist driven to distraction by a teenaged daughter and her friends. Tom Stoppard reviewing it in *Plays and Players* thought the problem was that it had not made the journey across the Atlantic. I think he was wrong – it had been just as bad in New York.

Once more the summons came from Hollywood to save my bacon. Would I play the dastardly villain Peter Thorndyke in *The Love Bug*? "Yes, please!"

Walt had died since I was last at the Disney studios but they carried on in his image. *The Love Bug* which really starred the lovable, sentimental little Beetle Volkswagen, Herbie, was the top grossing film in 1969 in the USA.

The children were growing up and at boarding school – except Henry, my youngest, who was six. A certain lack of discipline had crept into his life in my absence. The teachers at his school were commenting on his not infrequent use of four-letter words. The problem was that he had a tendency to explain: "My dad says that!"

Another episode involving Henry had already taken place at Swanbourne Primary School, run by Robert Smith, who was my idea of a perfect teacher and soon became a friend. Nice Mrs Viccars was in charge of the youngest group.

During playtime another child sought out Mrs Viccars to give her the somewhat dramatic news that Henry was swearing.

"What did he say?" asked Mrs Viccars, not very pleased as Henry was one of her favourites and sometimes stayed with her, always sleeping, to his delight, in a large feather bed.

The boy, eager to get Henry into trouble, spoke the dread word, "Bugger."

"Ask Henry to come in," said Mrs Viccars, and shortly Henry stood before her.

"Have you been swearing, Henry?"

Henry stood stock-still, making no response. She repeated the question. Slowly Henry nodded.

"What did you say, Henry?"

No reaction was forthcoming from Henry. Mrs Viccars repeated the question.

Again no reaction. "Aren't you going to tell me?" Again no reaction.

"Would you like to write it down?" This produced a fairly quick nod and a pencil and paper were produced. He wrote laboriously and handed back the paper. She was astonished to see that he had written: "F.U.K."

Poor Mrs Viccars, somewhat shaken, shot into Robert Smith's office to tell him. Robert phoned me immediately and it seemed to have made his day. It certainly made mine.

Henry and Audrey joined me in Hollywood towards the end of the shooting of *The Love Bug*. Within a short time, he was "cramping my style". The problem blew up at a barbecue held at the home of a friend soon after their arrival, with children and adults in abundance. I never like being interrupted when I am telling a story and was taking for granted the respectful silence while I held forth, when a small but unmistakable English voice was heard to say: "Don't fuck about, Daddy." The other kids looked bewildered as grown-ups fled in all directions choking on their hamburgers. When order was restored, Bill Walsh and Don Dagradi asked me if I would let them sign Henry up.

"I would rather hang him up by his feet," I replied.

If they were serious – and I think that they were, I have never regretted that decision. Talented children do not always fulfil the early promise they have shown. This can lead to frustration in later life. Such a fuss is made of them when they are very young. Later on, they go unrecognised. Some of the better-adjusted ones may welcome this. Years later, I was to learn that little Matthew Garber who had played the part of my son in *Mary Poppins* with such aplomb had died tragically young. I am led to believe that there was an unhappy element of drug abuse.

My last film for Disney was *Bedknobs and Broomsticks*. I always say that I got the part of the master wizard, Emelius Browne, because I was the only actor they could find who could sing under water.

Before I left for America, Maud Spector told me that she was likely to cast Bruce Forsyth in the role of a rather villainous character in the film. The idea seemed to be a good one. When Bruce arrived in Hollywood, it was explained to him what was required of him.

"We want you to do your trick with your hat."

"What hat?"

"You know, whaddya call it – the fez."

Bruce soon cottoned on to the fact that they seemed to think that he was Tommy Cooper. Disneys were not unduly perturbed when their mistake was pointed out by Bruce and he remained. Not long ago, one of my sons who had never seen the film when it was first released saw it at a matinee in North London. All the children shouted "Bruce Forsyth!" as soon as he made his first appearance in the film.

At the Dublin Festival of 1969 I finally attacked the classics. Peter Bridge produced an all-star revival of George Bernard Shaw's *On The Rocks* directed by Frith Banbury, and I played the Prime Minister, the longest part Shaw ever wrote and that is saying something. I enjoyed doing it and it was very well received. After Dublin, we played at Wimbledon, with the idea of going into the West End for a season. At Wimbledon, I'm pleased to say we did better business than Robert Morley had done earlier with Alan Ayckbourn's *How The Other Half Loves*. However, we folded. Bridge had gone bankrupt. Robert had gone on to the Lyric with Ayckbourn's play and stayed there for two years.

Breakfast at Brook Cottage – home then and now.

Empty-handed and unburdened for once in *Miranda* with Yvonne Owen and Margaret Rutherford.

Trying to look like Gary Cooper in *Helter Skelter*.

I had no idea we were making a classic – with Julie, Karen and Matt.

Flying without a plane for *Bedknobs and Broomsticks*.

Some special effects are easier for the actors – the football match in the same film.

The Love Bug – the public indeed loved Herbie the magical Volkswagen.

More wizardry for the Disney Studios.

We all enjoyed California. The whole family – Jamie, David, Willie, Henry and Audrey.

Willie – even at six he loved cars.

Willie presenting his handmade trug to the Princess Royal.

Directing Peter Sellers in *The Fiendish Plot of Dr Fu Manchu*. Our second film together – twenty-two years after the first.

Song at Twilight in South Africa – a wonderful role.

Luckier than most.

CHAPTER TWELVE

*In which
I do not succumb
to temptation...*

Since my first meeting with Robert Morley on the stage of the Lyric when he fixed me with a glassy stare, shot his cuffs and turned his back on me, our relationship improved. He was marvellous with old ladies and spent a good deal of time after visiting his own mother visiting my mother and charming her. I found him marvellous to work with, and always great company – but occasionally it was touch-and-go.

When I was in Hollywood making *Bedknobs and Broomsticks* he arrived, with a commission from *Playboy Magazine* to write an article about Vanessa Redgrave who was to protest about the Vietnam War. Vanessa had flown out from England with him, after some trouble acquiring a visa. The United States Government have always been a bit touchy about communism and one of their standard questions to a would-be visitor asked if they had ever been a member of any political group that could be affiliated with the communist party.

"Of course," Vanessa said.

But somehow she got her visa and she flew with Robert and her small baby to Hollywood. She was appearing in a reading of *Troilus and Cressida*, at a Los Angeles theatre but the high point of the evening was to be a protest – the protest was to encompass the Vietnam War, oppression of blacks, lack of rights for women and injustice in general.

Troilus and Cressida went splendidly. Vanessa has always been a marvellous, spell-binding actress and in my opinion there is nobody better. When the scheduled performance was over she announced that there would be a happening in the foyer.

"Ladies and gentlemen," Vanessa requested from the stage, "would you please go to the front of the theatre and watch and listen."

"This is it," Robert said, "come along. Don't forget, I've got my journalist hat on."

Outside the foyer some young people dressed in black and white were miming. It seems they were depicting life and death, justice and injustice – or whatever. It was all pretty incomprehensible. It didn't really matter, however, because the richly dressed departing audience was paying them not the slightest notice, so intent were they on getting away to various restaurants before they closed. Robert and I watched the protest quite alone before the police arrived, on cue, to break up the perfectly peaceful "demonstration".

We went backstage to pick up Vanessa. There were two notices on the board by the stage door. One was for a cleaning service and the other for family planning.

"How curious," I said, "you don't usually see adverts for family planning backstage."

"You do if Vanessa's in the company," Robert said.

The next day Vanessa was due to give a lecture at a church hall in what was purported to be an impoverished black ghetto. It was, she assured us, to be non-political. I was a bit nervous about what I was to find, expecting a west coast Harlem but we found the area more salubrious than Beverly Hills as many of the audience arrived in their Cadillacs to meet the famous English actress. After Robert and I set up the metal chairs which had been piled in a corner, Vanessa launched into a lecture which seemed to set out to prove that Sir Walter Raleigh and Francis Drake had started the Mafia. Every once in a while she punctuated the lecture with an Elizabethan madrigal on a tape recorder.

The audience was stunned. I'm not sure just what they had been expecting but this clearly wasn't it. When she asked for questions the silence was deafening. Finally a quiet voice was heard to ask, from a young black girl, "What are you smoking?"

Vanessa offered to share her harmless black cigarette. Her offer was nervously declined and that was the end of audience participation.

"Perhaps," Vanessa said, "Robert Morley would like to say a few words."

Robert good-naturedly took the stage.

"Vanessa is a darling girl," he began, "but she doesn't always get it quite right." He then proceeded to reduce the audience to tears of laughter with a few impromptu observations on life in California. He was careful not to go on too long – just long enough to give the audience the feeling that they had been entertained. They loved him.

He had persuaded me to drive him to Las Vegas. I've never understood or shared Robert's obsession or enthusiasm for gambling but I was intrigued by the idea of driving across the desert, so off we went. I was perhaps a bit over-enthusiastic. I was fined for speeding by a very polite cop. In Las Vegas we went to see the circus which was splendid and then we had a really good dinner at the Desert Inn which seemed even better when the head-waiter refused to take our money at the end of the meal.

"You are the guests of the boss," he said, eyes tilted upwards where it was rumoured the eccentric millionaire Howard Hughes resided on the top floor.

Robert then made for the roulette table. I watched him for about half an hour and then went to bed. I was woken the next morning by Robert marching noisily into the apartment. "I didn't wake you, did I?" He had not been to bed.

"Why doesn't your friend try craps?" one of the croupiers asked. "At least he would have some chance with craps."

Robert's reply was, "Do I have to explain to you too why I why I gamble?"

He just loves the spinning wheel – even when he has spent an entire night losing, as he had. It was Sunday night and I had to get back to work in the morning so I lent him some money to carry on and headed back to Los Angeles, determined to keep my eye on the speedometer. As fate would have it, I got a puncture. Miraculously, I was rescued by two policemen as good-natured as the one who had given me a ticket on the outward journey. In exchange for my autograph (for their children, of course) once they knew why an Englishman was in Hollywood they changed my wheel and escorted me all the way to my hotel. Next day I was back filming and Robert, I imagined, was still at the roulette wheel – losing.

Although I never could understand his interest in gambling I had grown to accept it over the years. The first time I came across it was during the run of *The Little Hut* when, rather suspicious of my flying skills, he bet me a hundred pounds that I couldn't get him to Le Touquet by noon on Sunday. Of course I did, although he wrote a totally false account of the flight, alleging that I mistook the coast of France for the coast of England. Nicole, a girlfriend of mine at the time, was with us – a witness to my accuracy.

When we arrived at Le Touquet Nicole and I went shopping while Robert headed for the casino. Later we went to find him there and lent him some money.

"You're going to have a go aren't you?" he encouraged.

"Certainly not," I replied, but Nicole thought I had better keep him company – and perhaps manage to set a good example if not keep him under control. I won thirty-five pounds.

"How wonderful," Robert exclaimed and then, realising that I was stopping, became horrified. "You're not going to stop now, are you? You're ahead."

"The best time to stop," I assured him.

I was furious when I read his totally false but funny account of the trip in a Sunday newspaper. I was quite unashamedly proud of my flying skills.

But a note arrived in the post. "Cheque enclosed. Sorry for the delay but my subconscious came to the rescue."

On another occasion he persuaded me to go to Cannes. It

poured with rain for a week. Robert hardly noticed as he was in the casino all the time, while I seemed to be constantly asleep under the flimsy air-mail edition of *The Times*.

On the Friday about eight thirty in the evening I was as usual fast asleep, *The Times* by this time on the floor in a heap, when Robert gleefully woke me up.

"Would you like some dinner, dear boy?" he asked.

I looked up. I couldn't believe it. Was I dreaming? Robert stood there joyfully holding two fistfuls of big square ones.

"My god," I exclaimed. "You've won."

"Oh, you are so dramatic," he said.

After dinner he proceeded to give back some of his winnings but not all.

Robert never managed to get me hooked on roulette. I'm much too keen not to throw money away, but he never stopped trying. He had slightly more success with another of his obsessions – racehorses. He had been to the Newmarket sales with his trainer, Farnum Maxwell. He bought a horse he later called Blue With Cold. That was all right but then he couldn't resist a little filly he spotted, which he later called Trample, and he bought her too, rather overextending himself. He rang me.

"David," he said. "You would like to have half a share in a horse, wouldn't you."

"Certainly not," I said, but he was not easily deflected.

"Would you rather have a half-share in one that cost two hundred guineas, or the one that cost fifteen hundred guineas?"

I fell for it. It would always be difficult to refuse anything to my old and generous friend. "The one that cost two hundred guineas," I said and found myself half-owner of Trample.

I have to admit it was rather marvellous. She won four times and was second three times.

Audrey only went to see her run twice – on the last occasion Trample was last and on the first outing at Wolverhampton she didn't even run. Someone had forgotten to bring her passport so she wasn't allowed to race.

"Just as well," Robert said, "it's far too cold for the poor little thing to run today."

Maxie advised that it would be a good idea to sell her in the December sales as the next year she would be very heavily handicapped.

"I don't like it," Robert said. He hated the thought of parting with her.

"You can have her in the back garden as far as I'm concerned," I said. Although it was fun having a winner I have never been very keen on racing. My father had become interested when he was a young man in Mildenhall. I sometimes used to go racing with him. He loved it but I only went because I liked to observe. Mrs Verney was a most distinguished, very aristocratic and quite elderly lady but, unlikely as it seemed, she had run Ladbrokes' "Book" on the rails for ten years in all weather.

My father would doff his hat and put on a bet using his pseudonym.

"Thank you, Mr Tomlinson," she would say, not heeding the pseudonym.

"What a funny thing," he'd tell me. "I hardly ever come racing but she always remembers me."

The truth was she saw him often.

It was very glamorous going to the December sales with a horse to sell and even more so when Trample was sold for many times what we had paid for her.

"I'd like to see who bought her," Robert said, showing the same concern as a father dispatching his daughter off to boarding school.

The buyer turned out to be an Australian. If you had passed him on the street you would have thought he might run a coffee stall somewhere, but he in fact had a gold mine in the Antipodes and was a millionaire several times over.

While I spent a good deal of time over the years avoiding getting involved with Robert's gambling he had no such qualms about getting involved with my efforts to raise money for Mrs Elgar and her autistic children. Sybil Elgar, quite rightly, always needed money. I took Robert to the school in Ealing. He immediately joined the children at their own level and began crawling around the floor in his best suit. He was as impressed and amazed by Mrs Elgar as I was. When she was talking to us, the children kept coming up demanding a cuddle from her. Autistic children, who actually can shrink from physical contact of any kind, wanted her to cuddle them – which of course she did unhesitatingly, no matter what they interrupted.

"Do you think she hypnotises them?" Robert wondered.

Mrs Elgar was devoted to these children. They were her life and she found it almost impossible to turn away a child she thought she could help. So she constantly needed to expand facilities – and that took money. Whenever I saw her the first thing she said was, "I need some money, you know."

"How much do you want?" I asked her on one occasion.

"Seven thousand pounds," she said without blinking.

I winced. Perhaps we could organise a charity show, I suggested.

"Nonsense," Robert said. "I can raise that in half an hour." And he did just that. He persuaded his friends to fund the venture. At a party he interrupted Lew Grade who was relating an anecdote at the time, to ask him for two thousand pounds.

"You'll have the cheque in the morning," Lew told him, "don't interrupt another time."

Lew started his story again from the beginning and the cheque arrived the next morning.

Robert had no hesitation in borrowing Mrs Elgar's begging bowl and returning it to her filled up, having of course added some of his own money. It never remained full for long though. Miracles don't come cheap and Mrs Elgar was in the business of miracles.

CHAPTER THIRTEEN

*Travelling
in Africa and
bidding farewell to
CST...*

In 1973 I was invited to perform in South Africa. My brother Peter was still living there and Michael had recently moved to Cape Town from Ceylon so there were two very good reasons for going. A third reason was William Douglas Home's play, *A Friend Indeed*, which I really thought deserved a greater success than we had achieved with it in London. It had run for about five months but only, it is said, because Willie kept pouring money into it in the hope that it would take off. Willie loves seeing his plays on stage, no matter what the cost. There was a fourth reason. I think South Africa is one of the most beautiful places on earth.

Audrey and I had acted there in the late fifties, really to visit Peter, and we were able to turn it into a working holiday. On this first visit the play we had decided to do was *Escapade*. This brilliantly witty play by Roger MacDougall was on in London whilst I was playing in *The Little Hut*.

"Now there is a part for you," Robert Morley had said, and I wondered if maybe he was trying to get rid of me. When I saw the play, however, I agreed with him and longed to do it and there was a part for Audrey. She agreed to play the mother of teenaged boys, although much too young for the part. Our own sons were just four and two at the time. We sailed from Southampton and spent the ten days at sea rehearsing. It was great fun working with Audrey. *Escapade* was the only time we acted together, although she had been an offstage voice in *All for Mary*, and played the maid in *Is Your Honeymoon Really Necessary?*.

At that time Peter lived in a very grand house with Sir Arthur Harris, his wife and daughter, and even then he considered South Africa his home.

It is true that, seductive as I found the country, I couldn't help but be appalled by the attitude of some of the people. I hardly ever saw a white man being polite to a black man and I never saw a black man being anything but polite to a white man. Everyone, no matter what colour, was very nice to us.

I did a special charity show of *Peter and the Wolf* with an orchestra conducted by Hugo Rignold and discovered the enormous difference between the theatre and the concert hall. In the theatre for a comedy, if you get four or five curtain calls that is quite enough. In the concert hall you never stop taking bows, but no one told me. I took my bow and left the stage for my dressing-room from which immediately I had to be fetched to return to the stage and acknowledge the seemingly endless applause. It is a curious convention and it is no wonder that some opera singers have such large egos.

There seemed also to be a never-ending social round – both backstage at the theatre where groups gathered after each performance and at people's houses where supper parties and drinks parties were constantly laid on. It was during that trip that we met Colin Cowdrey who was playing in a test match and my interest in cricket was re-awakened. He has been a friend ever since.

I was naturally very pleased to return to South Africa in the mid-seventies. Of course I found the social attitudes changing. Everyone admitted that there was still a long way to go and that the problem was very complex; but no one denied that change was inevitable.

A Friend Indeed had the success it deserved on this outing and what had been meant to be a brief run extended into months – including a tour to Rhodesia where from the stage, in thanking him for attending with his wife and family, I assured Ian Smith that I would personally carry any messages he would like to send to Harold Wilson. This received a deafening cheer from the audience and lengthy applause.

Audrey came out at the conclusion of the tour. This time our family was complete and all four boys were with us. We did a wonderful drive from Johannesburg to Sedgefield on the Indian Ocean where we had been lent a house. Later we drove along the coast to Cape Town. In anticipation I had been daunted by the prospect of the amount of driving we would be doing but in reality it was a delightful journey during which we met with nothing but friendliness from black and white alike. By this time Peter had bought his own house in Sea Point and from the sitting-room window if you were lucky you could see the flume from a whale, spouting on the horizon. It was a wonderful trip and I was more than pleased to stay on for more work after the family returned home. I can see nothing being gained from isolating South Africa – and probably a lot to be lost.

On the 1974 trip I played Hugo Latymer in Noël Coward's *Song at Twilight*. I thought it a marvellous play ever since I had seen Coward himself playing the bitchy, ageing, homosexual writer at the Queen's Theatre in 1966. That year I was in *A Friend Indeed* so I could only get to a matinee. When the performance was over I hurried along to the Cambridge Theatre to get ready for the evening show and found a message awaiting me from Cole Lesley, his secretary. Would I please ring Mr Coward at the Queen's Theatre. Though I knew him well I was quite surprised. Backstage when he had come to see *Dear Delinquent* he had said some nice things to me about my performance and the show. Also he was once quoted as saying, "David Tomlinson looks like a very old baby." Of course, I rang.

"Why didn't you come round and see me, dear boy?" Noël demanded.

"I hoped you would be putting your feet up between the shows. I didn't want to disturb you," I said.

"That is very considerate of you, but I would have liked to have seen you."

"I didn't think you would know I was there."

"I always know who is in front," he replied crisply.

At this time my eldest son David had just started at Lord William's School in Thame. Gerard Gould was the English master there. He was also stage-struck. Gould was very keen to mount a student production of Coward's play *Postmortem*. Noël had written it, an angry vilification of the First World War, in 1930 shortly after playing in R. C. Sherriff's *Journey's End*. Coward was astute enough to realise his play wasn't nearly as good and never allowed it to be performed professionally, although it had once been staged in a prisoner-of-war camp in Germany in 1943. Gould asked him if the sixth form at the school could do the play and amazingly enough he gave his permission. I thanked him for his generosity and tried to get him to come down to Thame with me to see the play but he couldn't face it. He was probably right. It wasn't a very good play but the boys performed ably.

I felt my performance in *Song at Twilight* was perhaps my best ever, although it wasn't as successful in South Africa as *A Friend Indeed* had been. Again, Audrey and the boys joined me and this time we visited the Victoria Falls and then travelled on to the Wanki game reserve. David, Jamie and Henry rose very early to go with me on safari for a glimpse of lion and elephant but Willie, though actually very adventurous, put first things first.

"Breakfast please," he said determinedly and Audrey stayed back at the hotel with him, while the other three boys joined me, rather bravely I thought, as just the day before our arrival one of the park wardens had been killed by an elephant.

Just as I was leaving for home I was sent the script of *The Turning Point*. I agreed to do it because I was so flattered to be wanted whilst still in South Africa. It was a very wordy farce, translated from the French, in which I was to play the successful writer of commercial light comedies who finds it difficult to take anything in life seriously. Anyone I wanted to direct it was unavailable, including Frith Banbury. In the end I had to direct it myself. The agony was shortlived. We opened at the Duke of York's and closed – not quite within the week, but jolly nearly.

I was involved in another French curiosity that year – a film called *Bons Baisers de Hong Kong* – a really bizarre experience. The plot involved the kidnapping of the Queen of England and starred a French woman who makes a living looking like the Queen. I played the Lord Chamberlain. I don't think it was ever released in this country, so no one noticed. Moreover, I learned something. I learned I didn't like Hong Kong. The whole cast and crew got food poisoning or pink eye or both which didn't help matters. This, coupled with terrible humidity, did not endear the place to me. I returned in less humid times to appear in *Hawaii Five-O* with Jack Lord, in my opinion one of the most arrogant and unappealing actors I ever worked with.

Just as I had found my grandfather a delightful, kindly, interesting character, so my sons enjoyed the company of my father. By the time they got to know him he had mellowed. My relationship with him by now was excellent and he relied on me. I marvelled at how he had coped with a very complicated life and greatly admired the way he bore, with stoicism, the natural infirmity that comes with age. CST never complained about his health although he often had cause. He did remain a philistine to the end, but he had always had charm. He retained his sense of humour. Perhaps he had changed over the years – and perhaps I had. My three brothers were abroad so it was natural that I should see a lot of CST. By now he was especially fond of me and he adored Audrey. He was also extremely proud of my successful life. "I must admit, I never expected it," he once told me. "I was wrong about you, wasn't I?"

My son David passed his law finals and I was very excited and proud and rang CST to tell him.

"Of course he has," Father said simply as if I had been

quite potty even to doubt the outcome. There had been no question in his mind that David would pass. He always felt a special bond with him – and now they were lawyers together.

Towards the end of his life, CST became preoccupied with famous trials of yesteryear – he had a fair collection of the series. The two cases in which he was particularly interested both involved women who were convicted of murdering their husbands. One was Mrs Maybrick who, although reprieved, served fifteen years. The other was Edith Thompson who was hanged. Both cases were thought to be a bit dodgy. When I asked CST what the most momentous event in his lifetime had been, he said without a moment's hesitation: "The wrongful conviction of Mrs Maybrick."

His dislike of the judges – themselves long since dead, of course – who had tried the two women, knew no bounds and became almost an obsession. Sometimes his memory would fail him and he would scrawl their names down in handwriting that was none too fluent but quite distinct.

CST had a soft spot for most women in trouble. In his ninety-fourth year, he got me to take him to the Stonehouse trial. He had little interest in Mr Stonehouse but his secretary who was charged with him was a very different story. CST rejoiced when she was freed by the judge, having spent several of the short adjournments in the case trying to befriend her in the canteen at the Old Bailey. In the early stages of the case I too had spoken to Stonehouse who was also on bail for a time. He was understandably rather preoccupied but remembered a time when he was a Minister in the first Wilson Government when we had met. We had attended an RAF function at the Dorchester and later gone to Annabel's with his wife and another Labour Member of Parliament who was somewhat the worse for drink. This MP was making some less than flattering remarks about Harold Wilson and was not unduly concerned about who overheard him. Stonehouse had tried to shut him up at the time. When I reminded him of the occasion and the Labour MP, he said:

"He was right about Wilson!"

CST had always been astute, so it was particularly sad that in old age his native wit deserted him when faced with "knockers" – that shady breed of antique dealers who come rapping on the doors of housebound, elderly, perhaps confused people who are also lonely. The householder unwisely lets them in, for a bit of company and a chat.

The knockers' first move is to offer a ludicrously high sum for a fairly worthless piece. In a particular instance recently which happened to a friend of mine (who should have known better) the knocker's eye fell on a china plate. It was quite nondescript and virtually valueless.

"Oh," he exclaimed, "I like that. I'll give you fifty pounds for it."

A fool and his money, my friend thought as the man peeled the notes off a thick wad. Only then did the dealer casually announce that he might by the way just possibly be interested in the corner cupboard. From its position in the room it was obviously unused and unloved and it was true that my friend had never much cared for it and had no idea of its value. In fact, the dealer had spotted it as soon as he entered the house – finding the piece to initiate his ruse had been the difficult part. But the tactic with the plate had worked as it usually did. He offered her forty pounds for the cupboard which my friend gladly, in fact eagerly accepted, having no idea that it was Dutch marquetry and worth two or three hundred pounds. But the knocker knew.

The above incident involves no criminal offence although most people would think the behaviour dishonest and contemptible but so long as the knocker does not hold himself out to be an expert, he has made no misrepresentation. However, these fellows sometimes go further. One trick is to persuade the unsuspecting elderly householder that their possession is riddled with woodworm. This involves bringing a maggot or two into the house and placing them strategically on the *objet d'art* while the old person's attention is being diverted; never a difficult undertaking. This device then leads to the owner parting with their property very quickly, sometimes under the impression that they have not sold it at all but that the nice man has merely taken it away to get it treated. In fact they have signed a receipt for consideration of the goods. There is no doubting that these actions are patently criminal but it is very often difficult to bring a case. If the knockers are stopped by the police and accused of going equipped (with the maggots) for cheating, all they need say is that they must have left them in the car when they went fishing!

These people very often have a despicable streak of self-righteousness and unlike many villains generally whinge when they are successfully prosecuted. They resort to every conceivable device to postpone proceedings as long as possible in the hope that by the time the case comes to trial their victims will be even more elderly and confused and unable therefore to give coherent evidence. The best result of all for them of course takes place when the aggrieved has died in the intervening period, the demise invariably hastened by their disagreeable and unwelcome experience, at least in the opinion of other friends and family. On one famous occasion two men were arrested soon after an old lady had parted with her property in similar circumstances. They were held at a police station and their car was parked in the police yard. It was the height of the summer and although the engine and radio were firmly switched off, the car started to hum strangely. Closer inspection revealed that it was swarming with bluebottles. The lid of the jar in which the maggots had been kept was not properly on and the jar itself had been missed by the police when they had searched the car. The maggots had hatched!

No device involving larvae was needed with my father. He had no use for antiques, never had had. Furthermore, a lot of the valuable things in the house had belonged to my mother's mother, and because of guilt CST had developed an antipathy towards her. He knew that she had never approved of him and in his heart of hearts he also knew that she had good cause. Sadly, out of loyalty, my mother accepted whatever CST proposed and for many years before her mother's death she never saw her or even communicated. For the rest of my mother's life she deeply regretted this.

On CST's ninety-third birthday Audrey, David and I drove to lunch with him at Folkestone. It was a warm and sunny day and when I walked into the sitting-room, there sat a man whom I at first thought was his doctor. On closer inspection, it seemed plain at least to me that he had Pentonville written all over him. While he had been sitting chatting to my father, his colleague was dredging the kitchen for whatever had been previously missed – a futile exercise as CST had already been cleaned out months before. Indeed, so anxious had they been to get their hands on some of the grandmother's things that they had even replaced some items with inferior rubbish. CST had expressed surprise that I had even noticed the difference!

Although it was my father's house, I ordered both men to leave forthwith and followed them outside. Of course they knew their rights and were content to give their names and produce their driving licences to support their identity. One in particular was as bold as brass. When David asked him if he came – as so many of them do – from Brighton, he replied, "Yes, and I am proud of it!" From the appearance of the contents of their car, they must have had a good day elsewhere. Characteristically, they whined when we told them that they were dishonest parasites. With little confidence that there was much else that could be done, I telephoned the local police.

It emerged that neither man was unknown to the police who were understandably cautious when I enquired specifically if either had a criminal record. Of course there was no further action that could be taken although the Detective Sergeant to whom I spoke, with infinite patience, later took the trouble to visit CST and tried to disabuse him of the notion that these men were nice friendly chaps. Of course

CST probably did not really believe that but pride and obstinacy precluded any possibility of an admission that he had been conned. "I suppose you are sorry that you won't be getting these things after I have gone," he murmured. We protested that the only thing that made us sorry was that he had sold his possessions for a bare fraction of their value. "I don't need to sell anything. I have plenty," he said plaintively and we realised that there was no prospect of any logical further discussion. The incident clearly preyed on his mind, though, because on at least one later occasion, he mildly rebuked me for expelling the men from his house! He looked too for support from Audrey and David but they told him in no uncertain terms that both men seemed to be rather unpleasant. Dear Mrs Matty, unable to hear what was happening, kept repeating, "They helped themselves to the silver."

However, there is some reason to think that many of these people live on their nerves and I have since learned that one of the two men we saw that day later committed suicide. I cannot believe for a moment, though, that it had anything to do with our rather turbulent but brief confrontation.

CST's doctor, for whom I had mistaken one of these men, had always seemed to me to be unpleasant . . . as well as totally useless. He was unable, or unwilling to help my father in coping with any of the ailments with which age or viruses had afflicted him. He just gave him whatever he asked for and after CST had stopped badgering him for certificates attesting to his competence to drive, all Father ever wanted was his sleeping pills.

During CST's last years I was constantly back and forth to Folkestone and it finally became apparent that he couldn't manage on his own any longer. Mrs Matty, despite her devotion, was nearly as old as he was and she couldn't cope either. One time I arrived to find that he had fallen down in the hall. He couldn't move and Mrs Matty couldn't shift him, so he had lain there until my arrival. Even I had trouble getting him into bed.

As I have said, his doctor was useless. He wouldn't even talk to Audrey on the phone. CST by this time had shingles and a painful urinary infection. Both had lingered for months and still he didn't complain. I suggested to the doctor that he might help us find a nursing home for CST in order for him to be medically assessed.

"That," he told me flatly, "is not my responsibility."

So, I began the search on my own, and a very depressing search it was. I was horrified by some of the places I saw – I wouldn't have put a dog in most of those so-called nursing homes – and the good ones were always full. I wasn't surprised by that – there were so few good ones.

Finally I found a home that seemed particularly suitable in an ironic sort of way. The house in Hythe which had belonged to CST's friend General Price (the father of Dennis who had found me my first London job understudying at the Queen's Theatre) had been turned into a nursing home. However, like all the others which would have been suitable, it was full. I rang the Matron again.

"We have a place for your father," she told me.

I was delighted and relieved.

"The only thing," she continued, "is we can't take him until four o'clock tomorrow."

I assured her that would be fine and began to make arrangements.

The next day the ambulance arrived at CST's house to transport him to the home. We were a little bit early, I thought, as I followed the ambulance up the well-manicured drive in my car but I thought also that perhaps Matron could not have meant precisely four. Fourish would do. I remembered going up the same drive many times in my youth to tea and parties and indeed remembered well the day Dennis had said, "I've heard of a job that might interest you."

We pulled up in front of the house behind a grey van and were preparing to get my father out of the ambulance when a rather anxious Matron appeared at the door and came down the steps towards me. She was afraid we would have to wait a while. As we waited we watched the undertakers carry a grey plastic bag from the house and deposit it in the van. The doctor who had been called to certify the death had been very late in arriving. We watched as the previous occupant of my father's room was driven away.

Twenty minutes later CST was in a warm and sunny room full of flowers – in the same bed that had just been vacated by the corpse. It was a very efficient establishment and twenty-four hours after his arrival CST's urinary infection had been cured. The Matron was marvellous and CST told her she had lovely blue eyes.

He was very well looked after in the General's old house and was very comfortable there. But as the days went by he began to get muddled.

"Where's my revolver?" was one agitated enquiry and another time he happily announced, "This is Buckingham Palace, isn't it."

Despite his growing confusion he always recognised young David when he visited. They were still lawyers together. David was in court in Maidstone and drove over daily.

Clarence Samuel Tomlinson died on March 5th, 1978. He was one month short of his ninety-fifth birthday. Today his descendants number fifty-eight, including the very latest additions to the family, my two granddaughters born within a month of each other in 1990. I thought back to a conversation we had had a previous Christmas when he had talked very openly about his life – about my mother and about Sophie and the children born into "the other side of the family".

"It was a sorry business," he had said. "But there it is. It is all over now."

CST was not a great film goer, but two films gave him unashamed pleasure and he would tell everyone how good they were. Both were about men who managed a successful life with two wives: *The Remarkable Mr Pennypacker* and *The Captain's Paradise*.

A month later Mrs Matty died. She was a very special lady. Loyalty had kept her going until she saw CST safely into his grave. He had always inspired that kind of loyalty in women, right until the end.

CHAPTER FOURTEEN

*In which
I work
one last time
with Peter Sellers...*

From time to time, throughout the twenty years since making *Up the Creek*, I saw Peter Sellers. I always hoped to work with him again of course. I thought him a brilliant actor. Peter became a tax exile and compounded the problems resulting from having a complicated personality by leading a complicated private life. Having been an overgrown, gawky and at the same time overweight teenager, who loomed over not only his fellow schoolmates but also his teachers, Peter seemed to spend the rest of his life trying to make up for his lack of adolescent success with girls by pursuing women with a vengeance. He defined himself by the women he could attain, the more beautiful, the more successful, the better. It was inevitable that he would fall madly in love with Sophia Loren when he made a film with her. That attachment signalled the end of his marriage to Ann, although Loren always maintained that interest had never been returned, let alone consummated and she didn't even mention him in her autobiography.

He rang me out of the blue from the Mediterranean where he was cruising on his yacht. Over the years, although keeping his interest in cameras (and by then video recorders) and taping equipment, his love of gadgets now extended to yachts, expensive cars and private jets.

"Would you like to make a film with me in Paris?" he asked.

"Yes, please," I said.

"The script will arrive tomorrow."

"Never mind the script," I said, "have they got any money?"

"They've got the money and I'll tell you what to ask," he said.

Indeed, they had money enough for me. Hugh Hefner, of Playboy Enterprises, was the executive producer.

For this movie, *The Fiendish Plot of Dr Fu Manchu*, Peter was to collect a million dollars plus a percentage of the gross. He needed that kind of money, as he had just spent five thousand dollars on a pair of eighteen-carat gold spectacle frames.

True to his word, as I always found him, the next day the script arrived – in, of course, a Rolls-Royce. Just the driver and the script in the Rolls. The petrol bill alone for the trip could have covered the housekeeping for a week. Why do movie scripts always arrive that way? It seems as if film producers have never heard of the post, which is probably why films seldom ever recoup their costs. Peter's policy was never, ever, settle for a percentage of the net profit of a film. There never is a net profit. Always, he believed, go for a percentage of the gross.

It was a "goonish" script, much influenced by Peter himself. It was about Fu Manchu's ("call me Fred – they did at Eton where I ran the laundry") plot to steal the Crown Jewels and involved a saxophone-playing woman police officer disguised as Queen Mary, a toy spider trained to steal diamonds and a flying Tudor-beam cottage in Wiltshire. On paper it was hilarious.

When I arrived in Paris I was rather shocked by Peter's appearance. Of course I had known about his heart attacks over the years and his pacemaker. He often rang me and did so when he was on his way to consult Christiaan Barnard in South Africa. Peter believed in going to the top – or at least to the most famous. But I wasn't prepared for what I found. He looked pretty grim. Having developed a stoop, he seemed to be smaller. Peter had always been concerned about his weight and since adolescence had dieted assiduously. Now

he was skin and bone. His head was skull-like – the skin
stretched taut. But he seemed to be, to me at least, his old
sweet self. He laughed and joked and did his funny voices.

Helen Mirren was in the film and Peter seemed fascinated
by her – as he was fascinated by most beautiful young
women.

"Peter took me out to dinner last night and we got terribly
pissed," Helen told me.

I pulled Peter's leg about this and I felt he was upset. He
rang me up very late that night.

"I don't think I'm going to like Helen," Peter said.

"Why ever not?" I asked.

"I don't like her going around saying we got pissed."

"Oh, come on, Peter."

"It's not very nice of her," he said.

Audrey, half asleep in bed beside me, murmured like a
roused dormouse, "He fancies her."

"Don't quarrel with Helen," I said.

"I don't think I like her."

"Peter, she admires you," I said.

At the first hint of praise his voice took on a different
timbre. "Really?" he asked, encouraging me to go on.

"She is absolutely delighted to be working with you," I
continued. "So calm down and don't get the wrong idea
about Helen."

All was forgotten the next day. Helen and Peter got on
very well and their friendship prospered. Eventually he
moved into my hotel, the Lancaster, with several other
members of the unit.

"Do you mind if I ring you sometimes?" Peter asked me.

"Not at all," I replied truthfully. "Ring me anytime at all."

And he did. He rang me very often. Usually at four o'clock
in the morning. He was an insomniac. But I never minded
because he was always amusing company even in the early
hours. We would have a cup of tea and then go downstairs
in the hotel where the old night receptionist was, as often as
not, lying asleep on the reception desk. We would have to

wake him up, to Peter's resounding fury. He should not, according to Peter, have been asleep on the job. He was, Peter insisted, paid to be awake. When the huge double doors were finally opened we would walk the streets until dawn. For some reason Peter was always cheerful with me. He talked to Audrey about his depressions but gave me only the good news.

At the end of the day we would often eat together and he was extremely funny in restaurants. We would go in and under his breath he would mutter, "The fucking French – they hate us, you know."

When the maître d' approached Peter would become most apologetic.

"You understand," he would say, "at least I hope you understand that Mr Tomlinson hardly knew Lord Nelson and I myself was only vaguely on speaking terms with the Duke of Wellington."

"Ah, Mr Sellers," came the inevitable reply, "you are so amusing." He would then lead us to the best table.

I never saw Peter behave badly. He never did in front of me, and I suppose I was flattered by that. He once exploded on the set at an actor whom he decided was trying to manipulate him in order to beef up his part. He gave him hell.

"He wouldn't have done that if you'd been here," one actor told me on my return to the set.

I was, of course, aware that he was capable of behaving badly, in fact, more than capable – actually prone to it, and I did think that he was terribly unfair to the producer of the film, who really did everything to try to make life easy for Peter. His name was Zev Braun. I liked him and everybody liked him – except Peter.

"I find him as pleasant as any producer I have ever worked with," I said.

"I don't like him," Peter said flatly.

"Peter, you must be logical. You cannot just say you don't like him without reason."

But Peter felt he could do just that. I failed. I simply couldn't get him to be nice to Zev.

It was of course an especially difficult time for Peter, although according to him his whole life had been especially difficult. He hated his childhood and found, he thought, a brief refuge in his first marriage. He dated all his adult troubles from the breakdown of his marriage to Ann. I do know he deeply regretted the end of their marriage for the rest of his life and often talked to me about her with affection.

Peter played two roles in the film – the Scotland Yard detective Nayland-Smith and Fu Manchu, the 168-year-old Oriental villain. For the first character Sellers wore no make-up except for a moustache but for the second the make-up was elaborate – long black fingernails, plastic to shrivel his cheeks, contact lenses to change the colour of his eyes. The make-up man was brilliant and he could do the make-up in less than ten minutes – which was just as well because Peter couldn't bear it. He had grown to hate filming and I believe that if he could have invented a way of making a movie without actually rolling the camera he would have done it. He no longer took pleasure from the process of acting. What he liked doing was the deal and he was a very clever negotiator. However, as far as his career was concerned, since the great success of the Pink Panther series, he was in a difficult position. He could more or less do what he liked – and that he, like Errol Flynn, found alarming. He knew if he made the wrong choice he had no one to blame but himself, and he agonised over the decisions he had to make.

That September, *Being There*, the film he had just finished was about to be released. He loved that film and his character in it, Chancy the gardener, so wise in his naivety. Peter had spent years getting that project off the ground and he pinned high hopes of garnering great acclaim for his performance. It was, I believe, his finest performance and I thought the film was wonderful. However, in the end, the Oscar eluded him and it was a great disappointment. He felt

Chancy was his masterpiece. He had no such confidence in Fu Manchu and demonstrated that by quarrelling with Zev and the director. The bizarre script was not translating to the screen with success and this was already apparent. In retrospect it is perhaps easy to see that it could have been marvellous on radio, just as the Goon Show was. The surreal images were best left to the imagination. Peter was both frightened and bored by acting at this point and lacked confidence in himself. I had no doubts. He was a great actor. Olivier had asked him to join the National Theatre.

"You will play all the classical roles," he told Peter, "and I can teach you to do them."

But Peter couldn't stand the boredom of going to the theatre every night. Boredom terrified him and I learned during those dawn walks that he needed someone with him to relieve his boredom. Hence the wake-up calls. Left to himself he just sat in his hotel suite and stared at the walls. He never read a book, never watched television, never went to a movie. Only to Audrey did he admit he was a manic-depressive. His behaviour was totally inconsistent. He would ring people up – organise to meet a large group which would then assemble at the restaurant he had chosen and Peter wouldn't show. He was afraid his friends would depress him.

Halfway through the filming Peter had another heart attack. He had been spending the weekend at his Gstaad chalet and was rushed to a clinic in Geneva. Zev Braun flew immediately to Switzerland. His genuine concern was not with the film but with Peter. He was appalled at the thought that he might die and he could not have behaved better under the alarming circumstances. Later, Peter perversely would not accept that Zev was genuinely concerned about him. Producers, according to Sellers, were incapable of human feeling and he was not pleased to see him when he came out of intensive care.

"I'd only like to see David," he curtly told Zev.

Filming was shut down for a month and I immediately got

on a plane to Geneva. Peter was sitting up in bed complaining about the nurses and the food and on my arrival he sent his loyal and exhausted assistant Michael Jeffries out for hamburgers. Peter astonished me constantly by popping pills into his mouth.

"What's that you're taking?" I asked.

"Oh, nothing," said Peter.

"No, seriously, what is it?"

"Valium," was his reply.

"Does Block [his consultant] know you're taking them?"

"Don't fuss, old bean," he said, "let's have a photograph."

Fully dressed I climbed into bed with Peter and Michael took a photo of us.

Peter was addicted to all kinds of patent pharmaceuticals and no one, friend, family or doctor, could convince him to stop taking them. But the hamburgers cheered him up. He was soon on the phone to Audrey, pretending to be Geoffrey Boycott, and so good was his impersonation she was completely taken in until he dissolved in giggles.

When the filming resumed Peter took over the direction himself. Of course, he was blamed for sacking the director.

"You can say I cut off his head, for all I care," he cryptically told a reporter who questioned him about it. The truth was that the decision had come from Hollywood. From then onwards when Sellers was in a scene himself, he put me behind the camera. We had a great time and I took it as a great compliment that he trusted me to check his performance.

"How was that, old cock?" he would ask.

"I'd do it again if I were you," I would say occasionally. And so he would, without question, but mostly he was perfect.

The following June he rang me from the Dorchester. He had stopped over briefly in London on his way to Los Angeles for a by-pass operation. I was appalled. He seemed to look forward to it. It is true to say Peter actually enjoyed the atmosphere of hospitals. Although he complained bitterly, he liked the attention. We arranged to meet in a couple of days. But in a couple of days he was dead. He'd had his final heart attack.

CHAPTER FIFTEEN

*Taking
justifiable pride
in the role of
paterfamilias...*

M y eldest son David is a barrister and sometimes, if I am lucky, he lets me into court to
watch him conducting a case, but usually he
discourages me from doing so. He says I am
a distraction.

Ever since my first visit with my father I have been fascinated by the law courts and I have attended many trials. The
first time my father introduced me to Serjeant Sullivan, the
great bearded Irish counsel whom he was briefing and who
may be best remembered for collapsing in court during his
defence of Roger Casement, he was charming and took the
trouble to spend time chatting to me.

David was lucky to start his career in pupillage with
Michael Corkery, QC. By chance, three generations of
Tomlinsons, my father, myself and David, were attending
the Stonehouse trial and Juliet Corkery was there making a
rare visit to court to see her husband at work. I have admired
Michael Corkery on several occasions performing with great
success at the Old Bailey where he was senior prosecuting
counsel for the Treasury, and on one notable occasion when
he prosecuted at Maidstone in what at the time the media
called the Satan case. I drove many miles each day to attend
the trial and it proved to be both fantastic and hilarious. The
defendant was charged with fraud in that he had obtained
large sums of money from wealthy unsuspecting religious
people in order to buy artefacts which he declared would
keep Satan at bay. One of the more unlikely artefacts was a

costly Rolls-Royce. The case was tried by Judge William N. Denison, QC, who seemed to me to control the case firmly but with the greatest modesty, grace and good manners – as good as, if not better than, anything I had ever previously heard from the bench.

Michael seemed anxious that the jury might acquit on the grounds that if rich people were idiotic enough to hand over large sums of money they deserved to be defrauded. I have since learned that barristers are prone to a fear of defeat almost as part of the job. But his fears were unfounded and the defendant was convicted.

Robert Harman, QC, another friend, on being called to the bar, was congratulated by an actor with the doubtful quip, "I hear you are joining the junior branch of the acting profession."

It was a fair joke but an absurd one. I have seen many brilliant advocates at work and the only similarity I can find with the acting profession is that the best of both make it look easy.

Actors learn other people's lines but barristers compose their own and they often need to do so, on their feet, thinking quickly with minimal time to decide not only on the right words but words that might prove crucial to the case. Acting is certainly easier.

My second son James is an actor and he is also an athlete. We have a special bond, I suppose, being in the same business. Jamie is wonderfully sensible, clever and practical – and he always was. He has marvellous hands and as a little chap he was and still is capable of dealing with any problems relating to a house or garden.

Henry, son number four, is also "in the business" on the production side and is successful. He is well liked and very efficient and it is my belief that he will probably end up as an impresario, employing us all – I hope.

Over the years our sons have warmed their parents' hearts. But certainly we have all taken the most pride in William's achievements. He, of all of us, has had the hardest struggle on the journey from being pronounced a write-off to being the hard-working, extremely gifted man he is today.

The obstacles he has overcome would defeat many of us but it is true to say that he is now, and has been for some time, the most organised, most occupied and most contented member of the family – with the possible exception of Audrey.

In 1974 Mrs Elgar left the school's premises in Ealing which she had outgrown and founded Somerset Court near Bristol. Her pupils were getting older and needed more space and more advanced facilities to continue their development.

Autism is a very severe form of mental handicap. Sufferers have an abnormal fear of social situations and they indulge in persistent compulsive and ritualistic behaviour. Some respond to the simplest change in their environment with terror. As children with autism grow into adolescence and adulthood their problems do not lessen – but in a specialised, structured environment they can be channelled into socially acceptable behaviour and indeed into worthwhile and useful productivity. Autistic people are often specially gifted and their skills can be developed. Many of the skills are formidable. There is one young man who can play any piece of music perfectly after a single hearing and another whose draughtsmanship is astonishing. A quick glance at the Houses of Parliament and he can draw it perfectly right down to the last detail. Many have special numerical ability and others are gifted artists.

Willie's talents are in skilled meticulous woodwork, drawing, painting and listening to music. His paintings are extraordinary and very imaginative. He also has an uncanny knack with machines ever since at the age of eight he took the motor mower out of the hands of Mr Tarbox, our friendly gardener. From then onwards if the motor wouldn't start it was always Willie who got it going. For years he did all the mowing – and we have a lot of grass.

Willie is clever, not to say astute. He is also totally

responsible for himself and fastidious in everything.

Thanks to Mrs Elgar he writes beautifully. He keeps a diary and is very conscious of the seasons. He also has a marvellous memory and he is fully aware of all that is happening. Lately he has taken to keeping in constant touch with friends and the family by telephone. When sometimes he cannot make me understand a word he has spoken he can write it down perfectly. Once frustrated by our inability to understand what he wanted he carved a wooden bottle and inscribed the word "piriton" on it. He wanted his hay fever pills and in requesting them had created a work of art.

Somerset Court is the first adolescent/adult unit of its kind in Europe. Mrs Elgar has retired but the work goes on. It is a pioneering and innovative place under the direction of Mr Bob Reynolds, a worthy successor to Mrs Elgar. Much progress has taken place since he arrived. There are now six individual houses and each person has his or her own room. Willie keeps his meticulously tidy. He is still very solitary and prefers his own company. When he is at home we generally see him only for meals, although he loves to know there are visitors in the house and nothing pleases him more than the sight of Uncle Michael arriving with a suitcase. He knows then that he will stay.

The need to be solitary is an important aspect of autism and is of course the most wearing cross the loved ones of autistic people have to bear.

All parents are very conscious of the future, the parents of handicapped children probably more so than most. The plan for Somerset Court is that the residents will continue to be a part of the community and will be there safe and sound in perpetuity.

Willie is always calm and gentle and his behaviour is perfect anywhere. He loves restaurants and is very interested in food. He can also cook a three-course meal. Of course he is handicapped and his remarkable progress doesn't change that. He has never been allowed out alone and needs a companion to cope with traffic, but what is miraculous is that thanks to so many people he is able to make the best of his life and to live it to the full.

Princess Anne came to Somerset Court in 1989 to open two new bungalows built in the ever-growing establishment. She accepted the compulsory bouquet of flowers and then she went on a tour of the premises, delighting everyone with her genuine interest and charming manner. It was a proud moment when, in the wood workshop, Willie presented her with a garden trug he had made for her. I watched as the boy who it was said would amount to nothing, grown now into a man, smiled at the Princess Royal and said, "This is a present for you, Ma'am."

It is true he had been coached to say the seven words but he said them well.

Professionally, I have lived long enough in the business to have played a wide range of characters, from heroes and amiable silly asses to dignified old gentlemen. For good measure I have even played a wicked villain, dying with a bullet in my chest in the back of a plane, the only time, as far as I can recall, when I wasn't basically a "nice guy".

It seems to me a remarkably full life that I have to look back on. Though everything is transient there has been so much variety crammed into it. It is something to have lived through two world wars, to have served in the Army and the Air Force (and professionally to have completed the cycle by playing naval officers on several occasions). I have weathered major tragedy and have had my triumphs and joys. Most of all I have had the blessings of a wonderful family life.

Sometimes I think back to Father's pronouncement that I would never succeed at anything. I remember the variety of schools where I never achieved much – the times of childish despair. I never quite dared to dream then that I would actually manage to earn my living in my chosen profession.

I may be sentimental but I can't deny that I have been luckier than most.

FILM CAREER

<u>1940</u>

Name, Rank and Number
Garrison Follies

<u>1941</u>

Quiet Wedding
Pimpernel Smith
My Wife's Family

<u>1945</u>

The Way to the Stars
Journey Together

<u>1946</u>

I See a Dark Stranger
School for Secrets

<u>1947</u>

The Master of Bankdam
Fame is the Spur

<u>1948</u>

Easy Money
Broken Journey
Miranda
My Brother's Keeper
Sleeping Car to Trieste
Here Come the Huggetts
Love in Waiting

<u>1949</u>

Warning to Wantons
Vote for Huggett
Marry Me
Helter Skelter
The Chiltern Hundreds
Landfall

<u>1950</u>

So Long at the Fair
The Wooden Horse
Hotel Sahara

<u>1951</u>

Calling Bulldog Drummond
The Magic Box

<u>1952</u>

Castle in the Air
Made in Heaven

<u>1953</u>

Is Your Honeymoon Really Necessary?

<u>1955</u>

All for Mary

1956

Three Men in a Boat

1957

Carry on Admiral

1958

Up the Creek
Further Up the Creek

1960

Follow That Horse

1963

Tom Jones

1964

Mary Poppins
The Truth about Spring

1965

City Under the Sea

1966

The Liquidator

1969

The Love Bug

1971

Bedknobs and Broomsticks

1975

Bons Baisers de Hong Kong

1977

Wombling Free

1978

Dominique

1979

The Water Babies

1980

The Fiendish Plot of Dr Fu Manchu

THEATRE
PERFORMANCES

1938
Arthur Brough Players,
Folkestone Repertory
The Merchant of Venice,
Queen's Theatre
[understudy and walk-on part]

1939
Northampton Repertory
Company

1940–41
Touring:
The Police Are Anxious
George and Margaret
Quiet Wedding

1950–53
Henry in *The Little Hut*,
Lyric Theatre

1955
Clive in *All for Mary*,
Duke of York's Theatre

1957
David in *Dear Delinquent*,
Westminster and Aldwych
Theatres

1958
John in *Escapade*, South Africa

1959
Tom in *The Ring of Truth*,
Savoy Theatre

1962
Robert in *Boeing-Boeing*,
Apollo Theatre

1964
Ralph in *Mother's Boy*,
Globe Theatre [also directed]
Bamber in *Trouble with Father*,
Northampton [also directed]

1966
Sir John in *A Friend Indeed*,
Cambridge Theatre
Dr Jack in *The Impossible Years*,
Cambridge Theatre

1969
Prime Minister in *On the Rocks*,
Dublin Festival

1973
Sir John in *A Friend Indeed*,
South Africa [also directed]
Hugo in *Song at Twilight*,
South Africa

1974
Philip in *The Turning Point*,
Duke of York's Theatre
[also directed]

INDEX